Strategic Investment
Decisions

Pearson Education

In an increasingly competitive world, it is quality of thinking that gives an edge – an idea that opens new doors, a technique that solves a problem, or an insight that simply helps make sense of it all.

We work with leading authors in the fields of management and finance to bring cutting-edge thinking and best learning practice to a global market.

Under a range of leading imprints, including *Financial Times Prentice Hall*, we create world-class print publications and electronic products giving readers knowledge and understanding which can be applied, whether studying or at work.

To find out more about our business and professional products, you can visit us at www.business-minds.com.

For other Pearson Education publications, visit www.pearsoned-ema.com.

Strategic Investment Decisions

Harnessing Opportunities, Managing Risks

LAURENCE KRANTZ AND ALLAN THOMASON

FINANCIAL TIMES
Prentice Hall

London	New York	San Francisco	Toronto	Sydney
Tokyo	Singapore	Hong Kong	Cape Town	Madrid
Paris	Milan	Munich	Amsterdam	

PEARSON EDUCATION LIMITED

Head Office:
Edinburgh Gate
Harlow CM20 2JE
Tel: +44 (0)1279 623623
Fax: +44 (0)1279 431059

London Office:
128 Long Acre, London WC2E 9AN
Tel: +44 (0)207 447 2000
Fax: +44 (0)207 240 5771
Website: www.business-minds.com

First published in Great Britain 1999

© Laurence Krantz and Allan Thomason 1999

The right of Laurence Krantz and Allan Thomason to be identified as authors
of this work has been asserted by them in accordance
with the Copyright, Designs, and Patents Act 1988.

ISBN 0 273 64153 0

British Library Cataloguing in Publication Data
A CIP catalogue record for this book can be obtained from the British Library.

This publication is designed to provide accurate and authoritative information in
regard to the subject matter covered. It is sold with the understanding that neither
the authors nor the publisher are engaged in rendering legal, investing, or any other
professional service. If legal advice or other expert assistance is required, the service
of a competent professional person should be sought.

The publisher and contributors make no representation, express or implied, with
regard to the accuracy of the information contained in this book and cannot accept
any responsibility or liability for any errors or omissions that it may contain.

10 9 8 7 6 5 4 3 2 1

Typeset by Boyd Elliott Typesetting
Printed and bound in Great Britain

About the authors

Laurence Krantz is a founder and Managing Director of Euro Log Limited, Europe's pioneers in formalised project risk analysis and management. In that capacity he introduced the practical application of project risk management in Britain, in 1975, working with North Sea oil and gas operators. A decade later he was instrumental in instigating and developing the first UK public sector initiative in project risk management through the Ministry of Defence Procurement Executive. Mr Krantz's ability to draw upon 24 years of personal and collective (Euro Log) applications experience across a broad spectrum of industries and project types has equipped him with a depth of insight and breadth of perspective in dealing with investment project uncertainties throughout the investment life cycle. Prior to founding Euro Log, Mr Krantz worked as a consultant with a marine planning consultancy, and with the US Department of Defense as a naval material scientific and technical specialist. Mr Krantz holds a BSc degree in Naval Architecture and Marine Engineering from the Webb Institute.

Allan Thomason holds an honours degree in engineering from King's College, London University, is a chartered engineer and has an MBA from Cranfield University, School of Management. He worked for several years with leading UK construction firms and for client companies, planning, designing and implementing major international projects, where he obtained in-depth experience of managing complex technical and commercial risks. He is now a chief consultant with Euro Log Limited and provides support to firms in diverse businesses in the oil, chemicals, pharmaceuticals, telecommunications and defence industries, facilitating improved investment decision-making and risk management. Through his work, he is interested in developing pragmatic practices for decision management by integrating and developing techniques and tools from diverse fields and widening their use by business managers.

Contents

List of figures

List of tables

Introduction

OBJECTIVES

Businesses pursue their aims through investments of one sort or another. Most have to commit resources in advance in order to provide a product or service for which they then seek adequate recompense. As old investments mature and business conditions change, new opportunities must be found if businesses are to continue to deliver future rewards. The discovery, selection and management of investments are fundamental processes for businesses and may often need to be repeated.

Most business plans face considerable uncertainties. Unfortunately, few opportunities exist that entail no risk or only minor risks, whereas there are unlimited possibilities of pursuing ventures with higher risks. Both the extent of resources required and the rewards realised may vary significantly owing to the impacts of the many risks that confront businesses. Severe risks limit the level of investor's returns and can even threaten the existence of a business, so that managing risks in the selection and execution of investments is critical to the success of every enterprise. If businesses are to exist and rewards be obtained they *must* invest and take risks but they must do so with great care. Investment risk management demands more than a haphazard approach.

Demands for rewards and attitudes to risk-taking vary and individual attitudes are often confused. High risk-taking is sometimes mistaken for entrepreneurship, so that only high-risk ventures are considered as 'real opportunities' regardless of rationale. The reality of all the risks combined can be overlooked and many a 'great opportunity' or 'grand scheme' has defeated a company when foreseeable risks have materialised. The guidelines in this book do not judge whether a company should pursue high- or low-risk ventures. We show how to assess which may be most applicable. The companies that will fare best are those that can increase the value of their opportunities while limiting the cost of their investments and the cost of the risks taken. This is the aim of good investment risk management and it is entirely consistent with the principles of entrepreneurship.

AUDIENCE

This book will provide useful guidance to a wide business audience involved in any of the stages of an investment, from strategy to selection, appraisal and execution. Typically, the roles involved in investment risk management include:

- chief executives and board directors;
- strategic analysts and planners;
- business and acquisition managers;
- investment analysts and planners;
- asset managers and key functional managers;
- project managers, planners and main project team members;
- business and project risk managers;
- management consultants.

STRUCTURE AND CONTENT

The book is divided into two major parts, as shown in Figure 1. The first part discusses the principles and process of investment risk management. The second part presents a methodology for risk management throughout the full life of an investment.

Fig. 1 Document structure

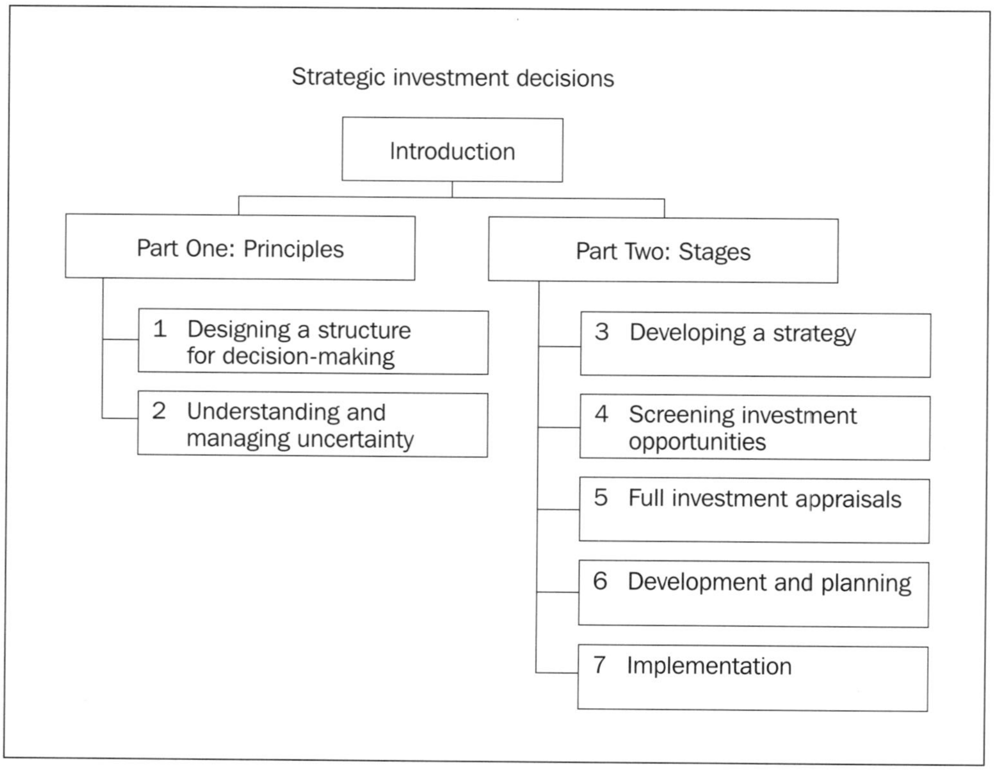

Part One: Principles

Here we discuss the need for defined procedures within a framework along with the management issues that must be addressed to guarantee their effective application. A generic framework is presented, founded on the logical sequence of investment stages, starting with strategy and ending with divestment. Then, the individual purpose of and principal activities for risk management in each stage are outlined, and a common approach to controlling objectives, activities and deliverables within each stage is introduced.

The essential principle is advanced that consistent objectives must be clearly stated and understood throughout all stages and the primary criteria against which a business should measure risk and reward are set out. General sources and attributes of opportunities and risks are considered next, followed by a review of major analytical techniques that may be employed. Part One ends with a view of standard strategies for responding to risk.

All readers should understand the principles set out in Part One of the book. Senior management particularly should consider the issues to be faced in developing, implementing and sustaining procedures for risk management.

Part Two: Stages

Part Two provides a practical guide to the objectives at each stage in the life of an investment and considers the specific procedures and tools to be developed and deployed to achieve those objectives. The guidelines provide a bridge from strategic analysis and the creation of investment opportunities, to the selection and appraisal of different options, design and planning, implementation, operation and final divestment of chosen ventures. They form an integrated methodology for investment risk management that allows businesses to obtain clear benefits:

- effective screening and selection of opportunities against strategic goals to avoid selection of poor investments;
- efficient use of management resources to reduce the time and costs of investment decisions;
- reduction of the potential impact of risks to increase the delivered value of investments;
- consistent application of procedures that improve communications, goal sharing, decision-making and confidence across the business.

If a man will begin with certainties, he shall end in doubt; but if he will be content to begin with doubts, he shall end in certainties.

Francis Bacon, *Advancement of Learning*, 1605

Principles

Designing a structure for decision-making

CHALLENGES FACED

The management of any business is rarely straightforward because businesses are faced with complexity, uncertainty and unplanned human responses.

Complexity arises from the number of issues that interact as well as difficulties encountered with individual issues. The number of issues and the levels of detail involved that must be analysed and managed require the employment of expert skills and a variety of techniques to achieve adequate control. However, businesses generally, or specific individuals involved with a venture, will not be as familiar with some issues or as skilled as others. Both the skills and tools may be unavailable, or there may be conflicting demands for scarce resources or a shortage of time, which frequently lead to errors. Resources change frequently within organisations and continuity can be lost. As a venture progresses, needs and resource requirements change. Staff change from those involved in setting goals to those who must create, evaluate and deliver opportunities. These aspects of complexity are then exacerbated by uncertainty.

Uncertainty arises because we cannot possess foresight about truly unpredictable issues and our information about predictable issues may often be incomplete or wrong. Even if we have good information, the ability to communicate it appropriately is frequently flawed. Our information about uncertainties may be poor so that we may not know all of the risks that might occur and we may not be aware of all the opportunities available to us. Businesses cannot know in advance which risks will materialise or how severely they will affect matters and, therefore, they cannot predict outcomes with certainty.

Human issues compound the problems. There are often pressures to pursue actions that are not consistent with stated objectives. Attitudes, confidence and motivation towards the tasks required, the goals set and the risks faced count greatly in dealing with them and determining outcomes. When presented with difficulties or confusion, people have a tendency to resort to dealing only with the issues with which they are comfortable or with those of personal interest. Personal objectives may prevail although they may not be visible.

AIMS OF STRUCTURED PROCEDURES

For every investment, a plan can be prepared to tackle both the specific issues and general difficulties to be faced, but most investments share many of the same issues and a unique plan on every occasion would be costly and wasteful. Instead, structured procedures can be designed that will provide a template for planning all investments, which may be applied to give consistently reliable results. The exact issues within each potential investment scenario will vary but the underlying stages and principles remain the same.

To be effective, it is important to select the right processes and to order them appropriately. The right processes are those that will handle the complexities and uncertainties involved while delivering focused analyses and solutions. To be efficient, it is important that the processes are applied, but only when and to the extent they are actually needed. Processes must not be over-complicated and a balance should be struck between qualitative and quantitative techniques. Both over- and under-analysis or *ad hoc* analysis and presentation can confuse decision-making and the wrong investment may be selected. Businesses must consider the trade-off between the benefits of decision management activities and the costs of their provision in time and money. Too much analysis or the wrong analysis can itself be inefficient or costly. With too little analysis, goals may not be properly set and the critical tasks and the risks faced delivering a venture may not be managed effectively.

Processes must also accommodate requirements for flexibility. Successful practice suggests that management procedures should aim principally to inform and assist management, by clarifying the objectives and deliverables required and the best methods available to achieve them but ensure that these guidelines are used as a benchmark. It then becomes a matter for practitioners to justify why they have deviated from the standard procedures, rather than to avoid variation when needed.

In all phases of investment, communication and the correct use of information is paramount. Communication must be effective in all directions: top-down to define goals and priorities; bottom-up to provide detailed knowledge of the business; cross-functional to give a balanced perspective of the business and the uncertainties faced. Companies work most efficiently when all sections of the company are heading in the same direction. Processes should encourage consensus wherever possible and ensure that understanding and acceptance of the reasons for decisions taken is achieved. If businesses do not consciously develop the procedural disciplines, coordination and skills required to improve decision-making across the business, confusion and poor performance will result.

> **If businesses do not consciously develop the procedural disciplines, coordination and skills required to improve decision-making across the business, confusion and poor performance will result.**

THE PRIMARY FRAMEWORK

Investment life framework

A whole-life framework for investments consisting of several stages, which will be familiar to most businesses, is described in logical sequence in Figure 1.1.

The stages also group into two broader phases, evaluation and execution. Evaluation must start with a clear definition of company strategy as all goals and appraisal criteria should stem from strategic objectives. These objectives should influence decisions for option selection, option appraisal and sanction and subsequent decisions within the execution phase. Execution involves the detailed project development and planning, implementation and operation of an investment if sanctioned. Later, the opportunities and risks faced in final divestment or reinvestment are also relevant in determining ultimate success.

> Evaluation must start with a clear definition of company strategy as all goals and appraisal criteria should stem from strategic objectives.

Fig. 1.1 Investment life and risk management framework

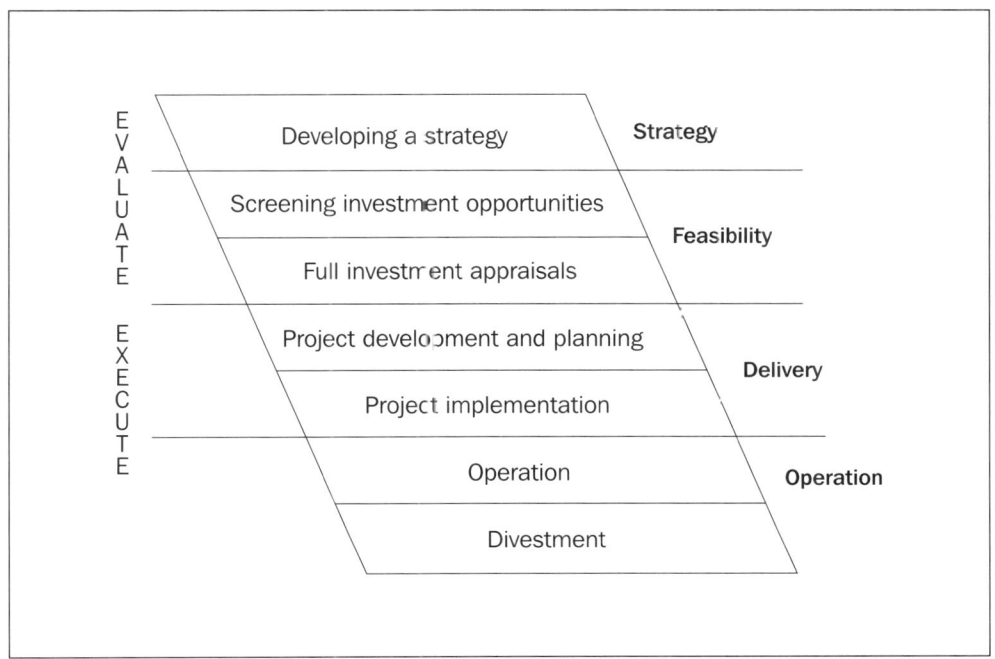

Management tasks vary between stages but the considerable resources of people, skills, information, tools, assets, relationships, time and money that flow within stages and between them in both directions must remain focused throughout on the same objectives and understanding of what is essential. Equally, processes and tools selected and developed to support specific analysis and management objectives must meet this broader aim. Such processes and tools must therefore be integrated within a consistent procedure that spans this framework and they should not be used in a piecemeal manner. Successful investments are not delivered by analysis alone and management of both objectives and risks must continue throughout the whole life of an investment.

> Successful investments are not delivered by analysis alone and management of both objectives and risks must continue throughout the whole life of an investment.

Introducing risk management to the investment framework

Continuity in managing risks throughout the life of an investment can be provided by the adaptation and use of generic risk analysis and management techniques across all stages. Emphasis should be given to the following:

- Qualitative registers (and/or equivalent analyses) should be used successively through the stages to capture uncertainties, risk responses and responsibilities, to prioritise analyses and management actions and to communicate information and decisions for use in later stages.

- Issues should be adequately explored qualitatively before detailed numerical analyses are conducted, but equal importance should be attached to the special benefits offered by Monte Carlo quantitative techniques to fully model most uncertainties.

- Full use should be made of those processes, techniques and tools that improve:
  - the definition of business goals and capture of critical issues;
  - the views and understanding of a business portfolio;
  - the identification and analysis of uncertainty and risks;
  - facilitation that aids decision-making by senior management;
  - the management of risks and the optimisation of opportunities.

The range of the principal processes and tools that are covered in this publication to assess and manage risks are shown in Figure 1.2.

Fig. 1.2 Principal processes and tools

Investment stage	Principal supporting analyses and process management tools		
	Qualitative	< >	Quantitative
Developing a strategy	SWOT PEST Market segmentation Competitor analyses Market demand analyses Value chain analysis Systems dynamics models Decision trees Scenarios		
Screening investment opportunities	Cost/benefit/risk register Value/preference modelling		
Full investment appraisals	Investment uncertainty register/reports Uncertainty appraisals		Risked DCF model
Project development and planning	D&P uncertainty register/reports		Risked project D&P plans
Project implementation	Implementation uncertainly register/reports		Risked project and contractor plans

The main processes and tools are summarised below. Details are covered in Part Two.

Evaluation phase

Stage 1: Developing a strategy

A company's strategy determines the general nature of the business and direction for that company, including both the types of products or services to be offered and positioning in the market place in terms of general pricing, branding, resourcing and supply strategies. Strategic risks and portfolio requirements must be addressed. Defining methodolgies for the development of a company strategy is not a main focus of the present book, but standard techniques commonly used for establishing the major objectives, factors, uncertainties and risks facing a business are discussed. These are required in order that a selected strategy and its attendant risks be communicated clearly and permit criteria to be defined that will determine whether investment opportunities should be pursued.

Stage 2: Screening investment opportunities

Early screening of opportunities against strategic criteria avoids selection of the wrong venture(s) and avoids unnecessary and wasteful expenditure of time and resources appraising inappropriate ventures. Screening should focus equally on the potential for increasing value and reducing risks as much as on valuing them. Particular techniques filter and prioritise different opportunities, and assess options against a portfolio view of the business, using visual qualitative tools. These include value preference modelling techniques, which engage a wider audience in early decision-making.

Stage 3: Full investment appraisals

Assessments now focus equally on detailed quantitative analyses of financial indicators such as Net Present Value (NPV) or the Internal Rate of Return (IRR) and detailed qualitative analyses which capture and prioritise the risks, risk responses and responsibilities and modelling requirements using investment uncertainty registers. Proper quantitative modelling of risks using Monte Carlo analysis techniques to predict outcomes as ranges of possible values and confidence levels to assess outputs offer an alternative to the simplistic use of discount rates. Terms for full or partial sanction of execution phases and setting of targets and contingencies draw upon this alternative approach.

Execution phase

Stage 4: Project development and planning

Management in the project development and planning (D&P) stage addresses opportunities and risks so as to reduce uncertainties for any investment, if full sanction has not been previously granted, while delivering risk-efficient development solutions and viable plans for implementing them. At the same time, risks to achieving the D&P stage goals themselves must be managed. The processes required now focus on traditional project risk management techniques, including the development of specific D&P-stage uncertainty registers supported

Early screening of opportunities against strategic criteria avoids selection of the wrong venture(s) and avoids unnecessary and wasteful expenditure of time and resources.

Quantitative modelling of risks using Monte Carlo analysis and confidence levels offer an alternative to the simplistic use of discount rates.

9

by Monte Carlo risk analyses of schedule, cost and resource plans to establish value-managed solutions.

Stage 5: Project implementation

In the implementation stage, uncertainty registers and quantitative risk assessments are now developed as tools for the proactive monitoring of and management action on risks, necessary to deliver project goals. Appropriate processes incorporate plans and perspectives on risks from within and outside the organisation.

Stages 6 and 7: Operation and divestment

The detailed techniques needed to provide the requisite level of identification and management of operational risks are not covered in the present text. However, maintenance of the uncertainty registers developed in preceding stages provides a useful facility to communicate and monitor the major investment and strategic issues that must continue to be addressed. An important task is regularly to assess options to reinvest or divest. However, these should be addressed against strategic needs in the same manner as any other investment option using the full complement of techniques referred to above.

INTRODUCING PROCEDURES

Developing procedures alone is insufficient; they must be applied consistently. Effective use will only be achieved if human factors are addressed and there is commitment to developing and applying procedures at the most senior level of management and across the whole organisation. The key factors are:

- attitudes to risk-taking;
- attitudes to analysis and use of structured procedures;
- structure and culture of the organisation.

Individuals have different attitudes to risk-taking and some enjoy taking risks more than others. For some, simply taking risks is more rewarding than the potential business returns, and many individuals find it is easier to gamble with others' assets than with their own. Ambition often encourages inappropriate risk-taking for personal gain, so that a proper analysis may be either discouraged or manipulated in order to avoid unwanted criticism and threats to personal stakes.

Alternatively, proper analysis may be discouraged because it is seen as too complex to conduct, too time-consuming, too costly or ineffective. Individuals may prefer to rely on intuition, 'gut-feelings', to determine their course of action.

Objections are understandable if the techniques used are inappropriate, have not been developed to suit the real needs or are poorly applied. It is true that a very few individuals can sometimes successfully weigh many complex factors without formal analysis. However, for most people, decisions based on intuition are commonly flawed because of bias and missing or misleading information, but the flaws are not always evident. Reliance on intuition usually indicates that the important issues are not properly understood and that the potential consequences of real uncertainties facing a business have not been thoroughly evaluated.

The structure, culture and leadership styles of companies can reinforce these attitudes and encourage a cavalier approach to investments and risk-taking. Risk-taking is often promoted by those who confuse it with individual entrepreneurship as a means to generate opportunities and success. Many company cultures therefore encourage an approach to risk that discourages planning or analysis and lauds the idea that all that is needed is someone who 'just gets things done' (often described as the 'John Wayne' approach). 'Getting things done' is also a major principle of good investment risk management, but the emphasis then is on first identifying and prioritising the right things to do before doing them. There is little value in getting things done if the wrong venture is being pursued.

Successful investment risk management is dependent on the right company culture being in place, so chief executives and senior management must take a major interest in the development and application of their procedures. They should show active commitment and support by championing both the procedures themselves and the right attitudes required. If company culture does not encourage a wider capture and sharing of critical issues with focused analysis that properly considers uncertainties and leads to rational decision-making, then companies should seriously consider changing their culture.

REVIEWS

An important aspect of using procedures is to review them periodically to establish that they are working effectively. Generally, a review should take place when the final outcome of a course of action first becomes visible, or earlier if a major unexpected event occurs. Although the timing will depend on the specific nature of the investment, it can usually be adequately predetermined at the sanction stage.

A review of risk management procedures should focus initially on the performance of the decision-making and risk management processes rather than the specific investment's characteristics. Specific project factors are always useful to learn, but they are not always repeated. Poor development of procedures and their inappropriate application are the primary causes of 'wrong' decisions and

> Decisions based on intuition are commonly flawed because of bias and missing or misleading information.

> Successful investment risk management is dependent on the right company culture being in place, so chief executives and senior management must take a major interest in the development and application of their procedures.

poor company performance against industry benchmarks rather than the features of the investment itself. The review should ask the following:

- Were the procedures applied throughout or were shortcuts adopted?

- Were adequate criteria properly established and communicated?

- Were uncertainties and risks adequately identified and assessed and rewards appropriately valued?

- Were the identified risks adequately managed and were procedures used to monitor developments associated with each risk?

- What changes to the decision and management processes could probably have improved the outcome?

- Would such changes improve control of other possible investments?

Management should not expect that they will always get the right outcome by having the right procedures. They will still need to take risks. Over time, the right outcome will be achieved more often if decisions are made for the right reasons than if the right outcome is achieved occasionally for the wrong reasons. As with any other area of business, decision-making and risk management can be improved continuously and businesses can enjoy increased benefits if the effort is made to do so.

Understanding and managing uncertainty

INTRODUCTION

A considered and structured approach to dealing with both risk and opportunity requires an understanding of the nature of uncertainty and aspects of its behaviour and influences that are relevant to managing business investment. This chapter begins with coverage of these aspects and then sets out a generic process for analysing and managing uncertainty throughout the investment life cycle. It concludes by relating the process to a sequence of practical responses to risk and opportunity. The subjects covered are:

- *Knowledge and uncertainty*   Discussion focuses on aspects of uncertainty and their implications for management. These include availability and validity of objective knowledge, use of assumptions, variability and uncertain events pivotal to investment viability.

- *A process for managing uncertainty*   A structured process is proposed for dealing effectively with uncertainty throughout the investment life cycle. The steps are grouped and described.

- *Managing risks and the risk process – the register*   Particular attention is given to the uncertainty register and other registers as analysis and management tools.

- *Qualitative analysis support*   The tasks and techniques involved in developing a qualitative understanding of uncertainties and their influences on an investment are described.

- *Quantitative analysis support*   This section addresses the value of quantifying uncertainty, risk and reward potential, and the considerations that should govern selection of modelling tools. It concludes with a discussion on principles of interpreting risk analysis results.

- *Managing risks and opportunities – actions*   Options and sequences for responding to risk and opportunity are examined and described, with specific attention to legal responsibilities and catastrophes.

KNOWLEDGE AND UNCERTAINTY

At its root uncertainty can be attributed to lack of knowledge. Unlike 'ignorance', however, 'uncertainty' implies an awareness of one's lack of knowledge, and with this awareness comes the possibility of remedy. But the reduction in uncertainty is neither an end in itself, nor does it equate to improved prospects. Figure 2.1 illustrates an instance where its diminishment brings bad news! Above all else, reduction of uncertainty is a means of taking more informed decisions.

On the assumption that every outcome in the form of an event or a result comes about through chains of cause and effect, a more complete knowledge of the causal mechanisms involved should be useful in reducing the uncertainty. Market research and preliminary design are but two examples of frequently employed means of reducing uncertainty through an improving knowledge of interrelationships. In most practical situations, however, a thorough knowledge of causal mechanisms remains a remote ideal. More imperfect means of simulating knowledge remain an inevitable recourse.

Management of uncertainty is about dealing in a methodical and effective way with known unknowns, the identifiable uncertainties, and the reasonably foreseeable.

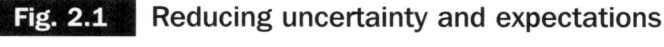

Fig. 2.1 Reducing uncertainty and expectations

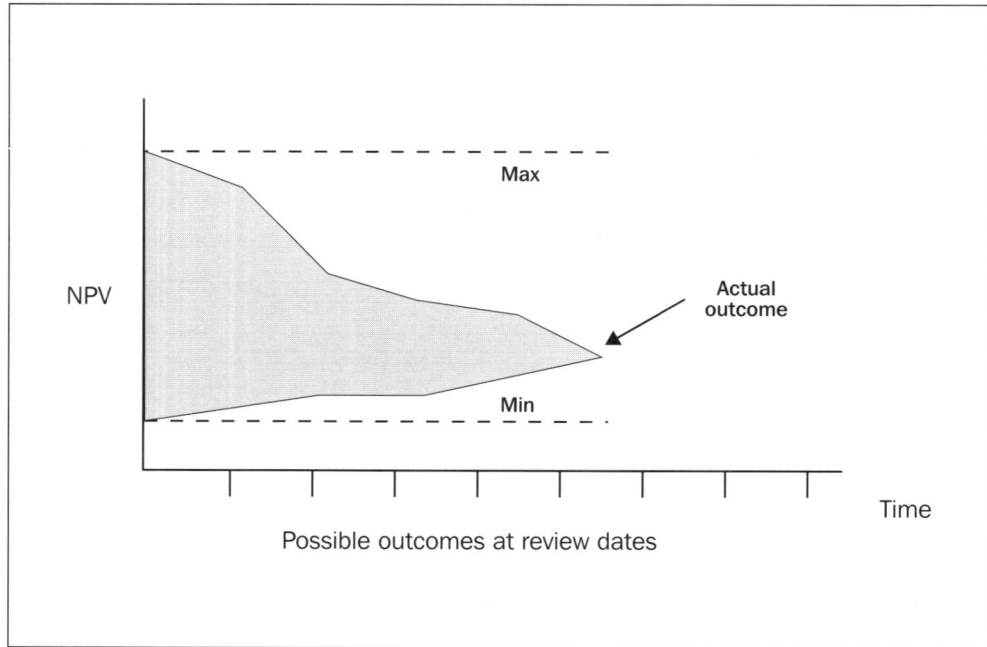

Unknown and known unknowns

Unknown unknowns are those uncertainties which, through an excusable lack of knowledge, are not even recognised as uncertainties. Unexpected physical phenomena which arise when designers venture beyond what they can reliably predict based on models of previous experience provide possible examples. Freak occurrences often highlight limitations in our knowledge of the causal mechanisms at work, which prevent us from anticipating or predicting with reliability.

Management of uncertainty is about dealing in a methodical and effective way with known unknowns, the identifiable uncertainties, and the reasonably foreseeable. Often we see a commercial or human disaster attributed by the media to 'unforeseeable' circumstances or conditions. A commonly cited demon is weather. Since no one can be held accountable for weather, like other 'acts of God' it is a convenient scapegoat for human failures. What is termed 'unforeseeable' weather usually tends to have been well within the boundaries of recorded experience! Where apology cites the 'unforeseeable', we can often read 'unforeseen'.

Most disasters are waiting to happen, with a number of identifiable ingredients conspiring to challenge the authenticity of the 'unforeseeable' label. For example, defective equipment due to poor maintenance practice is a frequent contributor to air, sea and rail disasters, as are poor or negligent operating practices and negligence. Changes to capital assets or their use which do not take into account the bases and limits of their design, limitations of users and influences from or on the operating environment, frequently emerge as dominant factors in disasters. All these examples involve foreseeable consequences, particularly when two or more of the ingredients are present to combine their influences.

Management responsibility is to take account of the likelihood that a situation might arise and the consequences if it does. The inability to identify and manage the unknown unknowns does not deny us the possibility of managing the known (or knowable) unknowns.

Relying on the past to predict the future

We tend to resort to experience to tackle uncertainty. It is the only reference for most of us. Predicting the weather on the basis of the most sophisticated analysis of past experience as recorded in vast data stores – we repeatedly get it wrong. North Sea mariners and offshore oil and gas veterans are not unfamiliar with the 'once in a hundred years' storm that occurs twice in one week! Extrapolation of design and performance curves for jet aero engines, again based on experience, failed to predict stalling phenomena which plagued the early larger commercial engines developed for wide-bodied aircraft. That which lay beyond the curves was completely unanticipated.

One might argue that in such cases, by a return to theory and 'first principles', by design could avert surprise by successfully identifying phenomena in advance. Nevertheless, historical data are often all we have at our disposal as means of roughly defining boundaries of expectation. To use them, however, without any attempt at understanding the differences between the influences operating on the current situation and those which prevailed to generate the outcomes previously recorded is to court deception and disappointment.

Benchmarking provides a popular and helpful means of comparing expectation with experience. History forms the basis for comparison, but used indiscriminately it can be limiting as well as misleading. Where industry experience has failed to realise achievable potential, benchmarking can perpetuate mediocre performance.

A good example of limiting beliefs is Roger Bannister's achievement of the four-minute mile in 1954. This set a record which was broken no fewer than 40 times within the following 12 months, when perceptions of limits had changed!

In trying to define the limits of future possibility, experiential knowledge is a convenient starting point. But history, benchmarks and norms are only guides, and should be used with care. Nevertheless, arguments for stretching the limits of experience should address convincingly the question of why or how this amounts to a reasonable expectation.

Assumptions and sacred cows

As an attempt to understand, the process of analysis often makes use of assumptions. Particularly in the analysis of situations fraught with uncertainty, the assumption provides a means of fixing selected elements or factors which, if allowed to vary, would eclipse and mask the combined influence of all other factors. As such, the assumption helps to clarify the behaviour and effects of other variable factors, many of which can possibly be managed or accommodated. It can be tested for its own influence by removing it or changing it, with everything else otherwise unaltered, and observing the results.

Assumptions also lend themselves to abuse as convenient substitutes for knowledge. Masquerading as facts and certainties, they become analytical sacrifices to management creed or fiat. Who among us is not aware of at least one 'sacred cow' in some organisation, which is never sufficiently challenged? Sacred cows seem to thrive wherever managements believe what they choose but are not sufficiently answerable for what they choose to believe.

A well known company had become almost wholly dependent on a single product line, production machinery for a specific industry. Displaced by a competitor in world sales, its management placed all their hopes on a new-generation machine aimed at the Chinese market. Historically, in Western markets, speed and low labour demands for operating and maintenance have long been cardinal attributes which determined primacy in the markets. The assumption of this 'truth' was so embedded in the corporate thinking that it was never questioned. Precious resources and time-to-market were squandered developing a machine uninteresting to a cheap labour market more concerned with robustness and simplicity of operation and maintenance than with speed and labour-saving features.

Assumptions may start life as legitimate aids to analytical clarity, being highlighted as limiting assumptions, caveats or conditions. With the passage of time and analytical handovers, perhaps more through lack of rigour than lack of integrity, their unverified nature is forgotten, and the assumptions take on the credibility of facts. Users forget to question them, or the assumptions become

History, benchmarks and norms are only guides, and should be used with care.

buried and forgotten in the sea of other information. They only come to light too late, when experience has disproved them, to a business's cost.

Variability and uncertain courses of events

In a statistical world of discrete events, where deaths, failures and losses either happen or do not happen, likelihood/probability of occurrence is a meaningful factor in determining where management needs to concentrate its greatest attention. It helps not only in prioritising and formulating actions but also in monitoring, at least qualitatively, the results of those actions.

In the world of projects and investment management, however, the likelihood of occurrence for an uncertainty is, for the most part, an invalid concept. It is not a probability that uncertain market demands for a speculative product will occur; it is a certainty. Computer programmer and labour productivities will be certain to be uncertain. Weather prospects will be uncertain, and the weather will vary. Specific definable weather conditions may be exceeded, and the likelihood can be statistically modelled. Likewise, if a key supplier should suffer financial failure, then further uncertainty is reflected in a range of possible severities of consequence. Here, too, it may be possible to put a likelihood on the event happening. But the great preponderance of uncertainties in projects and capital investments will not involve discrete events. They will be situations where one must contemplate a 100 per cent surety that there is uncertainty and that this manifests itself in variable performance prospects, better described as ranges of possible outcome than as either/or situations. Figure 2.2 depicts the two types of uncertainty encountered in investments and projects.

| **Fig. 2.2** | Discrete events and uncertain or variable performance |

If management is to understand and deal effectively with uncertainties in capital investments and projects, it must accommodate both kinds of uncertainty.

Uncertainty over time

If it is possible to wait long enough, most uncertainties will disappear. Unfortunately, in a practical world we cannot afford to wait for all possibles to become actuals before making major commitments.

We have already observed that the reduction of uncertainty does not *per se* bring good news. What is also useful for a decision-maker to bear in mind, when attempting to deal with the uncertainties confronting him, is that some of his most critical uncertainties will not diminish to any significant extent within the timeframe of his key investment or project decisions. These tend to be the global uncertainties outside his control and influence. Typically, their evolution from possibility to actuality yields little by way of helpful clues until long after the expiry of any useful decision options. Oil prices, exchange rates and other market influences are examples of uncertainties which may not diminish over the timespan of investment decision-making.

For such uncertainties the decision-maker must satisfy himself with understanding their influence on his enterprise and devising the best ways to accommodate them, to insulate his fortunes from any damaging influence they might have and use them to advantage where possible.

Other uncertainties, pivotal to the viability of a business or investment strategy, become certainties well into implementation or even later. They tend to relate to discrete events whose potential influences, but not outcomes, are foreseen from the early stages of planning. Examples include:

- public inquiries on infrastructure schemes;
- changes to political policy or regulatory regimes;
- results from tests of system prototypes or new drugs;
- results from oil and gas exploration.

With all of these examples, substantial speculative investment may occur prior to the events that will determine, or at least profoundly influence, investment or business viability. Decisions on that speculative investment may have to be incremental, each successive decision being based on a balance between:

- the cost of going forward with the next incremental commitment; and
- the current likelihood of a favourable event outcome, combined with the measure of potential reward.

Indeed, a decision to invest further in a specific scheme might well be justified on the basis of prospects for partial recovery of investment to date rather than ultimate returns on total investment.

A PROCESS FOR MANAGING UNCERTAINTY

The reiterative process

The adoption of project risk management received impetus as a consequence of many conspicuous failures to deliver projects on time and within budget. Several decades of practical experience in project risk management as a structured discipline have now produced a generic process which is extremely well suited to the management of:

- opportunity as well as risk;

- both these manifestations of uncertainty, throughout the life cycle of an investment.

As Figure 2.3 illustrates, the risk management process requires the integration of qualitative and quantitative analytical support in an iterative cycle of management activities through the whole life of an investment. These activities operate on a whole-life basis for each individual scheme and on a continual basis at the business management level. They are analogous to the activities which constitute management of project, or implementation, risk.

> The risk management process requires the integration of qualitative and quantitative analytical support in an iterative cycle of management activities through the whole life of an investment.

Fig. 2.3 The risk management process as an iterative cycle

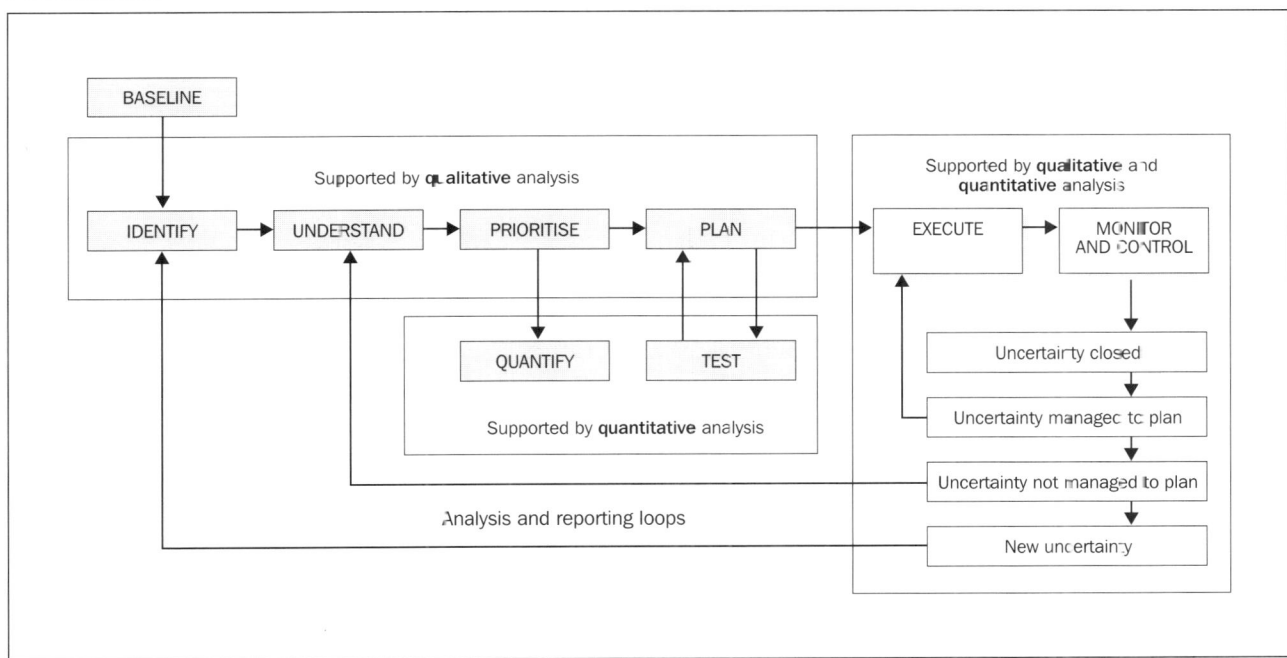

Supporting analysis

As Figure 2.4 indicates, the qualitative tasks that kick off an analysis of uncertainties should strive to achieve a consensus and a common focus, among the management team, on what is important in terms of risk and opportunity. Solutions-in-principle and personal accountability for the responses to individual uncertainties are additional outcomes of the essentially comparative analysis.

The quantitative analysis tests the insights and conclusions developed in the qualitative analysis by producing real dimensions required for most decisions.

Fig. 2.4 Risk analysis modes – their emphasis and uses

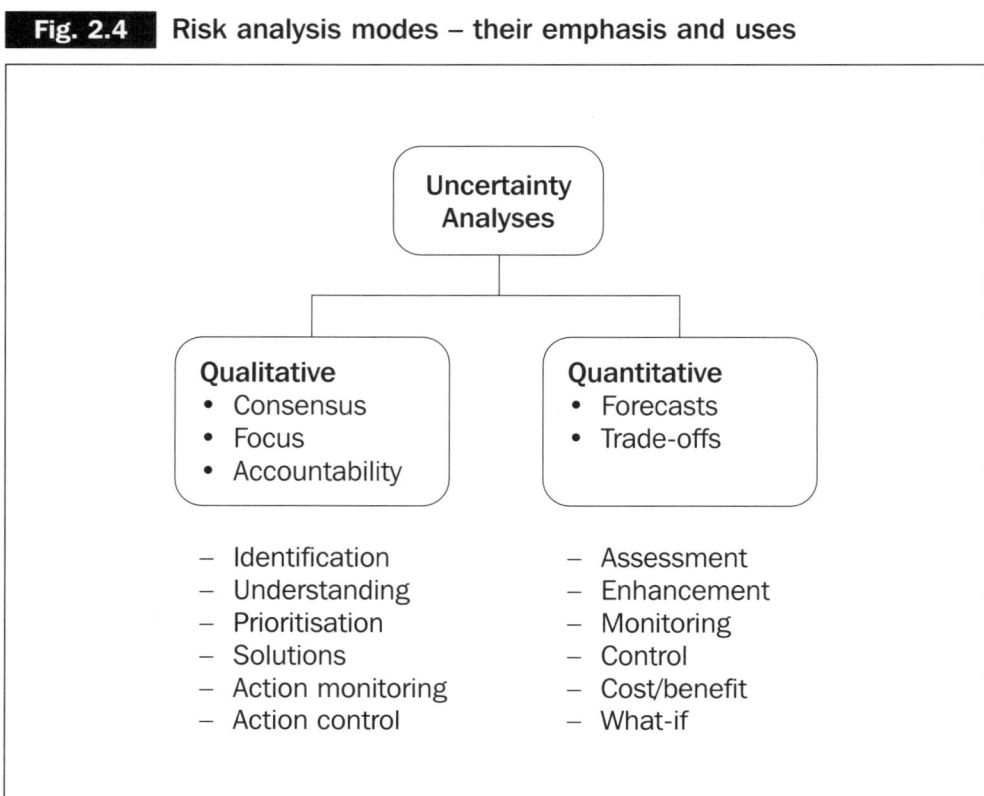

The quantitative analysis tests the insights and conclusions developed in the qualitative analysis by producing real dimensions (e.g. measures of time, cost, revenue and return) required for most decisions.

The steps

Baselining

A prerequisite to tackling uncertainty, with its risks and opportunities, is the clarification of terms of reference:

■ the content and boundaries of the individual scheme or investment programme being managed;

- the party from whose perspective risk and opportunity are to be managed;
- the objectives of the scheme or programme.

Although the establishment of a baseline will not precede every iteration of the risk management cycle, it should occur at pivotal decision points in the investment life cycle and at handover points where custody of an investment scheme passes from one management team to another.

Identifying

Identification of all known significant uncertainties relies on a structured approach involving various potential parties to a scheme. Typically, a brainstorming session or other collective discovery technique involving the management team starts the process by establishing a consensus as to the most important uncertainties. Importance is judged in terms of their influence on prospects for scheme cost, revenue, time and investment performance and prospects for meeting strategic objectives. Individual interviews by a facilitator with participants and any other designated key sources of information subsequently build upon the initial collective exercise.

Understanding, prioritising and planning

Both the group discovery activity and the subsequent individual interviews contribute to a structured analysis of the uncertainties identified. Such an analysis aims to:

- develop an understanding of each uncertainty, where it comes from, how it operates and the nature of its scheme and strategic influences;
- prioritise the uncertainties in order of their overall significance, in order to establish a common focus within the management team as to where attention should concentrate to reduce risk and improve opportunity;
- planning solutions-in-principle, for enhancing prospects;
- provide a focus for any quantitative analysis of uncertainty.

Quantifying and testing

While developing a common understanding, focus and solutions-in-principle, the management team can use the interviews to build up quantitative pictures of uncertainties and their influence on a proposed investment scheme or business plan. These views of prospects take the form of ranges of reasonably foreseeable performance with and without specific measures to enhance reward prospects.

The quantitative analysis often corroborates, but occasionally challenges, findings of the qualitative analysis, but it is more than simply a refinement of the qualitative work. Where the influences of uncertainty are significant, this quantitative analysis of prospects is invaluable in establishing realistic targets and achievable plans, and in testing alternative solutions to enhance prospects.

Executing

Executive action pursues the anticipated improvements for each selected enhancement measure. These measures to reduce risk and improve opportunity fall into two categories:

- measures to reduce the likelihood of adverse events or conditions or to increase the likelihood of favourable ones;
- measures to mitigate the impacts of adversity should it occur, or to maximise the impacts of favourable events or conditions which arise.

Examples of the first category are:

- alignment of ability to control, responsibility to manage and ownership of consequence in all scheme relationships where interests diverge;
- use of prototype or physical models for testing and validating innovative technology applications and designs;
- market research;
- public relations and marketing initiatives.

Examples of the second category include:

- insurance arrangements;
- contingency and fall-back plans;
- early development of claims defence systems;
- incorporation of sufficient design margins to accommodate enhanced production capacity if needed.

Some of the prospects' enhancement measures will be imbedded in baseline plans and budgets. Others will be activated upon the occurrence of predefined events or conditions.

Monitoring and controlling

By tracking progress in risk reduction and opportunity improvement, risk management becomes an applied management process rather than remaining an analytical activity. Most of the analytical and reporting vehicles which serve as decision-making aids in managing uncertainty are designed for progress tracking and accountability.

By tracking progress in risk reduction and opportunity improvement, risk management becomes an applied management process rather than remaining an analytical activity.

As a scheme is developed, is implemented and subsequently commences its revenue-producing life, many *uncertainties* become certainties and possibles become actuals. Whereas these initial uncertainties disappear, together with their attendant risks and opportunities, others emerge during the scheme's life cycle. Ongoing executive action and monitoring and control entail a repetitive application of the risk management cycle which captures these changes and facilitates:

- accountability for dealing proactively with major risk and opportunity issues;
- effective tracking of progress on those issues in terms of enhanced reward prospects;
- reliable tracking of certainty and risk levels on revenue, cost, time and investment targets;
- means of testing proposed decisions in terms of cost/benefit trade-offs, taking uncertainty into account.

Responses to what emerges during monitoring and control are shown as iterative loops in the risk management process (*see* Figure 2.3, above).

MANAGING RISKS AND THE RISK PROCESS – THE REGISTER

Managing the risks

The vehicle for storing and maintaining all qualitative information necessary for ongoing management of uncertainties and related risks and opportunities is the register (known as the uncertainty or risk register in project risk management). Information fields for recording progress on actions and their effectiveness render the register, in particular, an effective monitoring and control tool as well as an important contribution to a cumulative record of all management response to risk and opportunity. Risks registers provide a consistent means to communicate about risks throughout the whole life of an investment and to all management levels.

Numerous formats exist for uncertainty/risk registers, and several proprietary computerised database applications are commercially available for processing registers and tabular and graphical presentations of their contents. The more ambitious make the mistake of attempting to function as valid quantitative measurement tools, and some do not provide the necessary flexibility for users to define the information fields desirable for their particular applications. Those selecting database application tools for registers need to appreciate their appropriate

> Risks registers provide a consistent means to communicate about risks throughout the whole life of an investment and to all management levels.

uses, to anticipate their requirements for versatility. Figure 2.5 illustrates one example of a customised register format for uncertainty/risk item entries.

Fig. 2.5 A sample risk register record

RISK REGISTER

Client:	UK Industries
Project:	Asia

Date 2001

Risk ID/Title	A17c	Competitors build new plants leading to overcapacity
Description		Perceived growth in market may lead to similar new plant builds by competitors leading to overcapacity and reduction in market price

---

Source	External	**Phase**	Operation
Area	Industry	**Risk To Whom**	Corporate

Impacts		*Impact Scores*
Revenue	Planned utilisation reduced and market share and pricing affected	High
Costs	–	–
Time	–	–
Performance	–	–
	Likelihood	High
	Overall Score	6

Influence	Low		
Risk Reduction	Conduct marketing demand and competitor analysis to reduce uncertainty.		
	Investigate historic trends. Model/simulate variability.		
	Develop signalling strategy to deter rogue investment.		
	Consider JV options to reduce competition.		
	Delay/accelerate build?		
Cost	£ within appraisal budget	**Effect**	–
Manager	Regional Business Manager		

Modelling	Link separate analysis in risk model as variable inputs

Managing the process

So far, we have referred to the uncertainty register as a general analysis and management tool. Through the whole life of an investment scheme, different types of registers are employed for different purposes and at different management levels.

Figure 2.6 depicts the various business and stage-level registers that operate at different stages in the investment's life.

Fig. 2.6 The life cycles of investment based registers

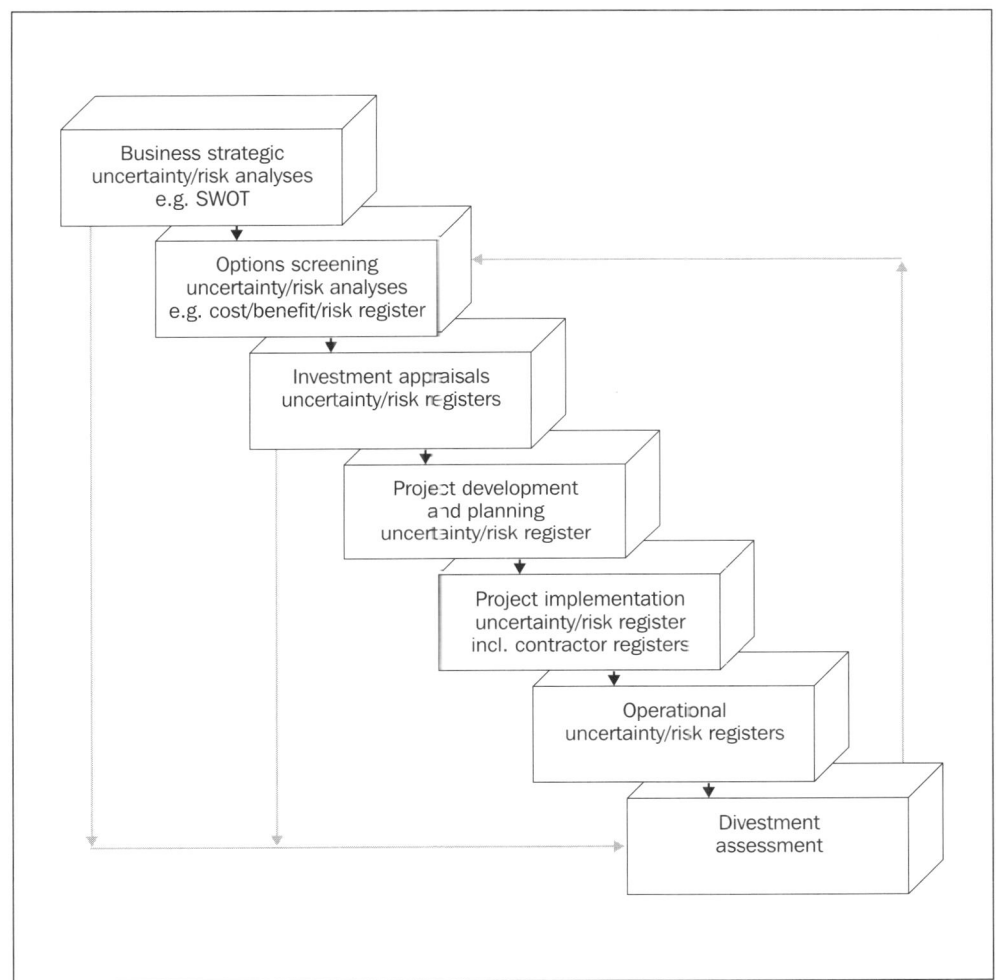

Stage-oriented registers act as management aids both in preparatory efforts which in some cases occur prior to stage commencement and during the stage work itself. Implementation, operation and divestment stages, in particular, benefit from the focus and proactive measures developed during previous stage preparations. Implementation involves the most intensive stage management use of its uncertainty register.

This is entirely consistent with hierarchical planning and a form of control more commonly associated with implementation stage management. During implementation, contractors are frequently required by the customer to develop and maintain their own work plans and programmes and uncertainty/risk registers. Internal task teams and subcontractors, on the other hand, are more likely to have the freedom to exercise their own judgement as to the need for registers at their levels.

In all applications of hierarchical uncertainty risk registers, as for hierarchical work planning and programmes, consistency is a cardinal rule. Information on uncertainties which influence not only achievement of objectives at the level where they are managed, but also achievement of objectives at higher management levels, must flow through to those higher levels.

For example, a development and planning uncertainty register might include a risk that mathematical modelling of a system's performance will be inconclusive, and that, as a consequence, more expensive physical or even prototype testing will be required. Clearly, this would be a specific risk to development and planning objectives as well as schedule and budget targets. It might also pose a profound threat to overall investment objectives. Procedures must, therefore, ensure that the uncertainty attached to mathematical modelling, wherever it first appears, is registered with its respective significances in both stage-level and investment-level uncertainty registers.

Information on all uncertainties which influence achievement of objectives at higher levels of management must, understandably, flow through to those levels. This is achieved through risk management reporting as prescribed in the risk management plan. Analysis of those uncertainties, with their selected risks and opportunities, at the higher management levels enables senior management to respond by communicating to subordinate levels the broader and overriding priorities for dealing with identified significant uncertainties. Where these priorities, defined by risk scores, differ from those dictated by lower-level objectives, subordinate levels of management can adjust their own priorities to accommodate the broader overriding ones.

Chapters 4 to 7 refer to the registers in use during the stages from Stage 2 (screening investment opportunities) onwards. In Chapter 6, the use of registers to communicate between management levels will be discussed with respect to the implementation stage where coordination throughout a management hierarchy is a matter of paramount importance. Chapter 4, in particular, describes the costs/benefits/risks register which accommodates cost and benefit factors as well as uncertainties in the screening process. Although the functions and make-up of this register differ from the uncertainty and risk registers, it shares with them its primary features as a permanent record of:

- knowledge and assumptions, at points in time, with respect to uncertainty and its influence;
- factors underlying management decisions and actions.

QUALITATIVE ANALYSIS SUPPORT

The critical discovery step – identification

Practitioners and users of quantitative risk assessment are no strangers to the benefits that such assessment often produces by exposing areas of major risk that previously have either gone unnoticed or have been noted but not given adequate consideration. The reason is that quantitative risk analysis forces them to think in terms of uncertainty rather than just risk. If, in the first place, we do not define the underlying uncertainties which give rise to areas of risk (or enhanced opportunity), how can we expect analysis to find the risks for us? We need to look first at the uncertainties themselves, not the risks. Thorough qualitative identification of uncertainties including both risks and opportunities is, therefore, essential to the proper assessment of investments.

An added benefit of this approach is that it avoids starting the exploratory process of analysis with the negative concept of risk. Enhanced opportunity can thus enjoy, from the outset, something more deserved than the lip service it receives from traditional risk analysis and management treatment. Opportunities for exceeding expectation can share management attention equally with threats to realising it. Let us begin by attempting to identify uncertainties that might have either a negative or a positive influence, or both, on achievement of the objectives and goals we have established.

Group techniques for aiding discovery

Brainstorming

Once we recognise the identification of influential uncertainties for what it is, a process of discovery, it becomes easier to appreciate the need to draw upon collective as well as individual knowledge, experience and creative thinking. The process of identification must consequently employ elements of spontaneity in the interaction between participants and structure – a classic case for brainstorming.

However, inappropriately managed or unmanaged uncertainty brainstorming can be (and often is) an ineffectual and wasteful expenditure of resources. It should not attempt to emulate the classic form of brainstorming used for creative applications such as the generation of ideas for product innovation or promotion. This classic brainstorming is, essentially, a 'right-brained' activity; it draws upon the brain's right hemisphere with its capacity for imagination, intuition and spontaneity. It aims at generating as many ideas as possible for subsequent screening. Used for identifying influential uncertainties, it tends to lack sufficient selective focus. The result is often the generation of too much that is trivial or

> Thorough qualitative identification of uncertainties including both risks and opportunities is, therefore, essential to the proper assessment of investments.

29

insignificant, with too little time left for screening and concurrence on grading and prioritising in the open forum. Uncertainty brainstorming, undertaken to support project and capital investment decision-making, ties up valuable management time and, therefore, must be structured to employ management's time efficiently.

Hence the need for drawing upon the 'left-brained' capacity for systematic method, analysis and evaluation in uncertainty brainstorming. Constant reference to established objectives and goals, maintenance of a consistent (overview) level of detail, use of prompt lists and checklists as *aide-mémoires* by the facilitator and critical screening during the identification process all contribute the elements of structure necessary to ensure the productivity needed. The discovery of influential uncertainties thus becomes a 'whole-brained' brainstorming, effectively a channelled form of spontaneous collective and individual effort.

Brainstorming achieves its most effective and comprehensive discovery of uncertainties and their influence through a good facilitator and a broadly represented but sufficiently contained (preferably fewer than 20 participants) group. The facilitator will use his skills to both stimulate and constructively channel spontaneity and creative thinking, and to drive discussion towards consensus. He will also recognise the point of diminishing return and ensure that the session ends up with a manageable number of uncertainty issues for analysis and action (normally fewer than 40).

Nominal group technique

Risk management has its proponents of alternative group-based identification techniques likewise applicable to uncertainty discovery. Principally, these include the Nominal Group Technique (NGT) and the Delphi technique. The skilled facilitator will employ aspects of brainstorming and NGT to suit a particular group and situation.

NGT is a variant of brainstorming. It seeks to overcome possible bias and the stifling of ideas in any group that can result from the presence of a few dominant individuals whose personalities or positions tend to intimidate the more faint-hearted participants. Each group member records a number of risks (within, say, 10 minutes). Then each, in turn, briefly presents one risk until no more are forthcoming. At this point, the members of the group individually score each risk – the scores are then amalgamated to reach consensus scores (and, therefore, a consensus ranking). The facilitator may introduce anonymity by the collection and presentation of recorded uncertainties, but this will have the inevitable consequence of extended session time.

Delphi

The Delphi technique provides anonymity for the faint hearted. The technique is used for risk identification or assessment by selecting a qualified group and asking them to identify and score risks. Opinions are given anonymously and without referral (allowing remote sessions, for example by e-mail). The coordinator then summarises the responses and elicits further input. The process continues until a stable and consensual opinion is reached. The lack of personal interaction for debate and clarification and for resolving conflicts is a severe drawback to this technique. Where distances preclude group sessions, however, it does provide a better-than-nothing substitute.

Interviews

Interviews function as a follow-up to the group-based discovery techniques. Their primary purpose is to develop further understanding of the uncertainties identified and their influences, and to explore appropriate management responses. The dialogue of the interview, however, frequently brings to the surface additional uncertainties as sources of significant risk or opportunity. This is not surprising, since the interviews involve individuals selected for their in-depth expertise relevant to particular uncertainties identified in the group forum.

Analysis for understanding and prioritising

Analysis of uncertainties and their influences is useful only to the extent that it either improves the reliability of forecasting or helps management to improve the outcomes that are forecast. Unfortunately, there is always a limited availability of management resources and many competing demands on them. This imposes the need for selectivity and prioritising of analytical effort and management focus.

Two potential pitfalls await those setting about a structured scrutiny of uncertainty, risk and opportunity. The most frequent mistake of project risk analysts, and the failure most widely criticised by the decision-makers they support, is the spawning of oversized and unmanageable inventories of risk issues. There can also be a strong temptation to use the structured evaluation techniques suitable for qualitative analysis to produce quantifications of risk. Indeed, many analysts and risk management practitioners refer to the comparative scoring of risks as quantitative analysis! Lessons from experience with the results of both mistakes are clear:

■ confine each managed uncertainty/risk inventory to a single overview level of detail for each level of management;

■ confine each inventory to a number of uncertainties/risks which the management team involved can deal with and monitor effectively;

> The most frequent mistake of project risk analysts . . . is the spawning of oversized and unmanageable inventories of risk issues.

- accept qualitative evaluation techniques for what they are, a means of understanding and prioritising uncertainty issues and assessing orders of magnitude; don't try to use them for quantifying ranges and certainty levels for possible performance.

Focusing on risk

The group sessions convened for identifying influential uncertainties normally extend their effort to achieving a consensus on the scoring of those uncertainties. In risk analysis this amounts to the rating of each uncertainty in terms of its risk significance. Whether completed in the open session or during subsequent interviews or group review, scoring of risks becomes a means of monitoring the 'top 10' or most important risk issues and tracking progress in risk reduction.

Figure 2.7 illustrates a typical risk matrix scoring system where likelihood of occurrence or significance is combined with scale of adverse impact to produce a score for each risk. In this case the scale is 1 to 6 in order of ascending importance.

Fig. 2.7   Example of a risk-scoring matrix

Probability			
High	2	5	6
Medium	1	3	5
Low	1	2	4
	Low	Medium	High

Impact

Scoring of risks becomes a means of monitoring the 'top 10' or most important risk issues and tracking progress in risk reduction.

By populating each box with the IDs and names of risks with that corresponding likelihood and impact, the matrix becomes an easily interpreted picture of a project's or investment's risk profile. The shaded boxes towards the upper right contain risks flagged for priority attention. Typical of scores obtained from these matrices, this one displays a deliberate bias in weighting for impact. The heavier weighting of impact amounts to recognition of the importance of being able to survive consequences of any risk should it materialise.

Table 2.1 indicates the types of management action considered appropriate to each level of risk (risk score). The example used is intended to accommodate both opportunity and risk-generating uncertainties.

Table 2.1 Type of management action by significance score

Likelihood of occurrence/significance	Impact severity	Score	Action indicated
High	High	6	Requires essential allocation of resources where there is scope to clarify or enhance prospects.
Medium	High	5	Requires priority allocation of resources where there is scope to clarify or enhance prospects.
High	Medium	5	
Low	High	4	Allocation of resources for further assessment or prospects enhancement desirable if available.
Medium	Medium	3	Uncertainty identified and included in Prospects Management Plan.
Low	Medium	2	No serious influence anticipated but requires tracking. Identify potential measures in event of increasing risk or decreasing opportunity significance levels.
High	Low	2	
Medium	Low	1	Routine reporting and tracking to ensure no adverse trend in significance level.
Low	Low	1	

The grading of likelihoods and impacts relies on clearly understood criteria for definitions of 'High', 'Medium' and 'Low', established and agreed beforehand. Table 2.2 is an example of qualitatively defined grading criteria.

Table 2.2 Example definitions of likelihood of occurrence/significance and of impact severity

Likelihood:

High	Risk almost certain to occur.
	Schedule with no margin and/or based on estimates for which no proven metrics exist.
	Cost estimates based on high-level tasking, or estimation without experience from previous similar programmes.
Medium	Risk likely to occur.
	Schedule based on experienced estimates but little margin available.
	External dependencies which allow little flexibility.
	Cost estimates based on low-level tasking or with experience from previous programmes.

Low	Not a serious risk.
	Schedule based on demonstrated experience.
	No external dependencies.
	Cost estimates based on detailed analysis.
	Contractors prices where the work is clearly defined.

Impact:

High	If this risk materialises, targets will almost certainly be missed.
Medium	If it materialises this risk is likely to impact on targets.
Low	If this risk materialises targets are not likely to suffer impact.

A more positive focus for management

If we wish to allow for any uncertainty to be either a source of risk or a source of opportunity, or both, we can easily adapt established project risk management convention (in the form of the risk matrix) to reflect both sides of the coin. At the same time, in allowing for risk and opportunity for each uncertainty, we provide a framework for accommodating both uncertain events and uncertain or variable performances. The uncertainty mirror matrix in Figure 2.8 caters for the uncertainty whose range of possible impacts straddles expectation, as well as the pure risk generator.

Fig. 2.8 The uncertainty mirror matrix

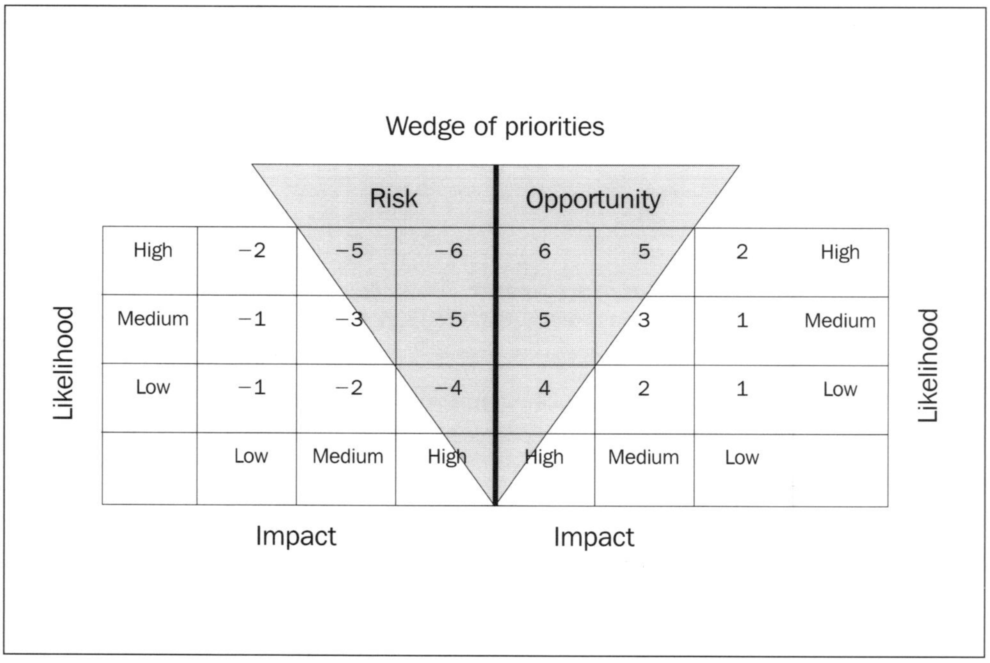

The symmetrical presentation concentrates management priority within the central wedge of the matrix. Thus, with minimal additional effort needed to grade those uncertainties which have significant upsides, we produce a more balanced and positive focus for practical initiatives.

Refining the focus

The risk and uncertainty grading we have looked at is both subjective and crude. In particular, it might be argued that the uncertain or variable nature of an uncertainty's impact makes any single grading of that impact as 'Low', 'Medium', or 'High' a distortion of that uncertainty's true significance. For instance, a low-probability exceptionally high rainfall during the growing season might be more significant as a risk to crop production than a medium-probability heavier-than-desired rainfall. The answer might be to use the applicable likelihood/impact category which produces a higher score on the matrix.

Particular impacts from an uncertainty are often of much greater import than others. For instance, schedule impact from a possible technological breakthrough might be far greater than impact on development cost. The general practice is to use the highest graded impact for overall scoring, although uncertainties can be scored separately for various types of impact for the purpose of formulating specific management actions.

Whenever we are tempted to further refine our scoring of uncertainties, we should ask ourselves if we are attempting to use qualitative analysis to produce quantitative measures. If the answer is yes, or even maybe, we should direct the benefit of doubt, and our efforts, to proper quantitative analysis.

> Whenever we are tempted to further refine our scoring of uncertainties, we should ask ourselves if we are attempting to use qualitative analysis to produce quantitative measures.

Analysis for planning, execution and quantification

Analysis, beyond that needed to prioritise management attention, should be confined to that work necessary to support measurement of uncertainty and its influences and to develop actions to:

- prevent adversity or mitigate its impact;
- capture extra opportunity or exploit it.

Table 2.3 lists some of the aspects of uncertainty which typically figure in its qualitative analysis, and how they are used.

Table 2.3 Aspects of uncertainty useful for the development of management responses

Aspect	Management use
Phases/areas affected	Indicative of the timing and location of potential risk and opportunity impacts, and suggestive of the nature of measures to influence them.
Impact descriptions/orders of magnitude	Means of describing, grading and monitoring potential impacts of the uncertainty.
Likelihood of occurrence/significance	Means of grading and monitoring the likelihood of risk or opportunity arising as a significant influence on outcomes.
Ownership	Central to the principle of aligning controllability with ownership of consequences.
Potential for influence (e.g. nil, influence, control)	Central to the concept of proactive management and the prioritisation of management attention. Useful for checking alignments of controllability, responsibility and ownership of consequences.
Risk reduction and enhancement options (incl. costs)	Facility for identifying and selecting measures available for reducing risk and capturing and enhancing reward potentials.
Management responsibility	Means of establishing accountabilities for progress in risk reduction and improvement in business performance potential.
Action dates	Practical facility for triggering management action with an urgency appropriate to the risk or opportunity.
Related assumptions	Facility for recording and tracing key assumptions underlying information developed on the uncertainty.

QUANTITATIVE ANALYSIS SUPPORT

Dimensions for decisions – risk models

Decisions in projects and capital investment programmes inevitably involve trade-offs of risk and potential reward, cost and benefit. 'Soft' benefits and drawbacks may enter into decision-making, particularly as strategic considerations, but the decisions will be largely 'dimensional', i.e. based on quantitative measures.

This is where the quantitative modelling of uncertainties and their interactions becomes indispensable. The structured evaluation techniques and other methods of qualitative analysis discussed previously help to prioritise and formulate management responses in principle to risk and opportunity. They cannot reliably measure either existing outcome prospects or the trade-offs of proposed management actions in the presence of significant uncertainty.

In 1998/99, scientific modelling of uncertainty took something of a beating in the field of global investment banking. Losses in Russian bonds and in LTCM's (Long-Term Capital Management) hedge fund called into question the methods of assessing market risk. Criticisms of portfolio risk modelling cited its understatement of likelihoods of extreme events and its use of flawed assumptions relating to the causal mechanisms which generate market price.

Yet what was the direct response to these events? International banks and bank regulators committed to improving quantitative modelling and its application where weaknesses were recognised. The reason is simple. Whatever its imperfections, modelling addresses the need to quantify and control risk. Without modelling, investment banks would run the danger of taking on too much or too little risk, and failing to achieve the returns necessary for their survival.

For capital investment and project programmes, where both risk and opportunity for enhanced reward place similar demands on business, quantitative uncertainty modelling is essential to support decision-making. It is where project risk management began – because of the need for better numbers at the time of commitment. Nothing has changed. Project and investment risk modelling have always presented difficulties and demanded high levels of skill for yielding valid and reliable depictions of real life with its interrelated uncertainties.

Modelling tools and skills

Investment and project risk modelling have fostered the emergence of numerous mathematical techniques and tools based on Monte Carlo simulation. Decision tree and influence diagram techniques, sensitivity analyses, spreadsheet-based simulation tools and stochastic project activity network (CPM)-based tools abound in sufficient numbers to require considerable expertise in order to select the right tools for each business purpose.

The demand on modelling skills and the selection of appropriate modelling tools for various functions relating to investment decisions, commercial support and implementation management are now important issues. As in all uncertainty modelling, the considerations involved assume a logical order. Figure 2.9 sets out these considerations as a sequence of questions, the answer to each of which drives the answer to the next. As the diagram indicates, modelling skills should be dictated by all the other considerations; they must not – as is too frequently the case – be the determinates.

Of course, it is also important for the custodian to distinguish between genuine considerations and non-considerations. Figure 2.9 includes, for illustration, two of the most frequently misused examples of the latter.

Fig. 2.9 **Considerations in modelling uncertainties**

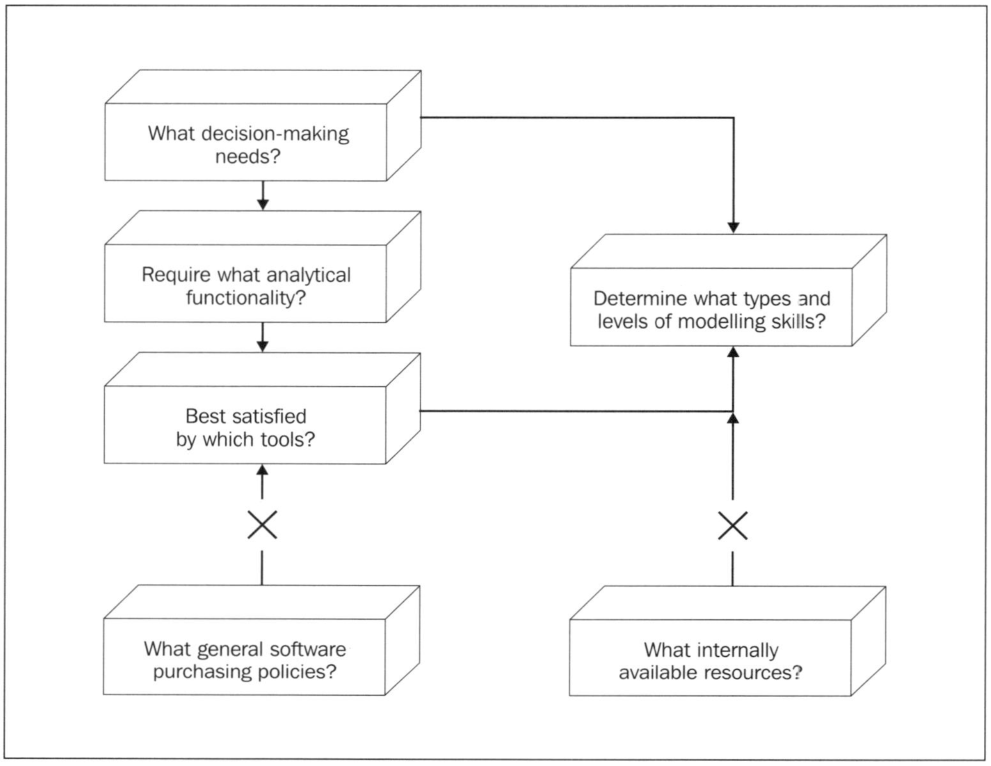

Quantitative analysis of investment and project uncertainty can and should draw upon established best practice in project risk management. Modelling and estimates of uncertainties draw upon the qualitative analysis developed for each uncertainty recorded in the uncertainty register. Thus each uncertainty in the register is 'mapped onto' the model(s), and there is an information field in the register for that uncertainty, describing how it has been modelled. The modelling recognises the relative importance of each uncertainty, as indicated by its score, in the level of attention given to its treatment.

Nature of a risk model

A risk model uses Monte Carlo simulation techniques and dynamic modelling to represent all major risks and general estimating variability including time. Dynamic modelling means that when a factor is changed all related factors in a model will also vary; this avoids manual intervention and scenario assessment when used in conjunction with simulation modelling.

In Monte Carlo simulation modelling, all significant input variables are represented by ranges of values rather than a single estimate, wherever appropriate. These ranges are frequently approximated to triangular distributions defined by minimum, most-likely and maximum values. Other assumptions and risks may be represented by special distributions or by conditional and probabilistic branching in the model. Risks are mapped from the risk register to ensure that full coverage of all major risks is included. After sufficient iterations in a simulation which selects different input values and possibly different scenarios in each iteration, a plot of the many different possible outcomes is produced in the form of a distribution curve. This approach is shown in Figure 2.10.

> In Monte Carlo simulation modelling, all significant input variables are represented by ranges of values rather than a single estimate.

Fig. 2.10 Monte Carlo modelling method

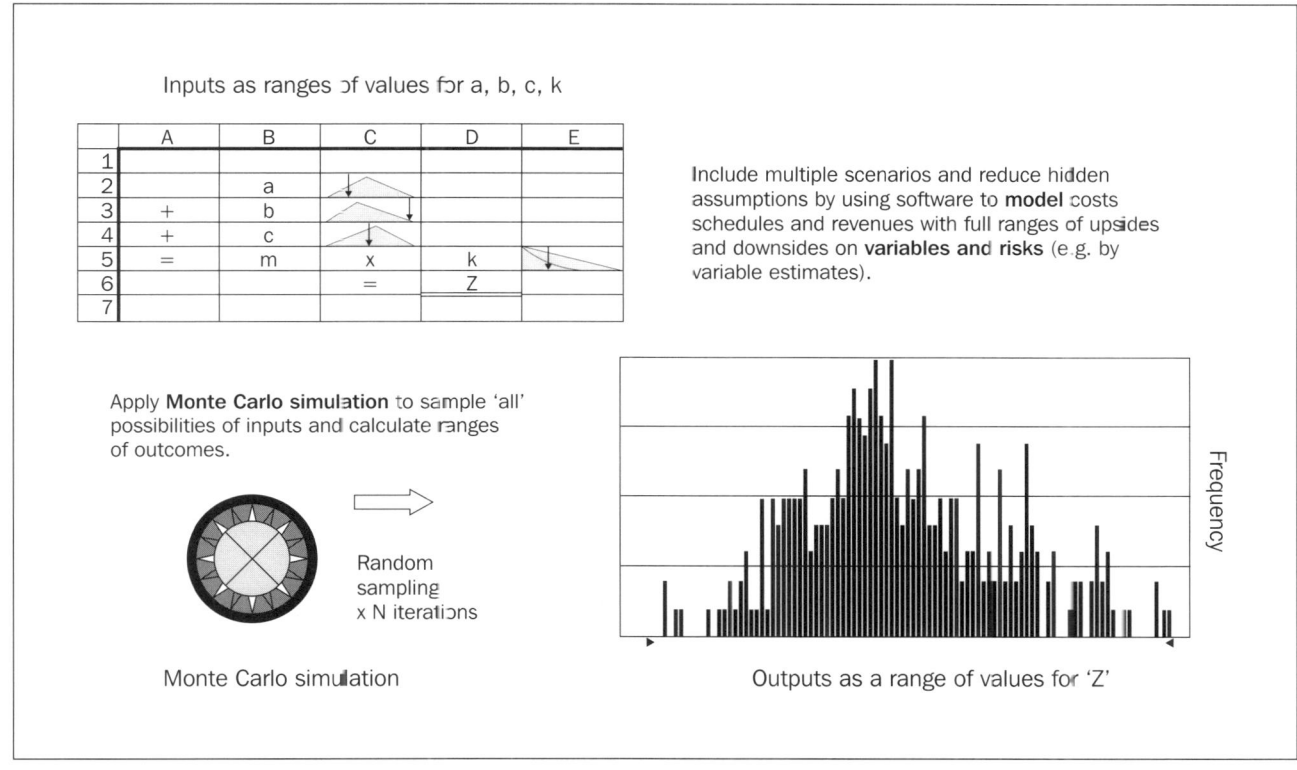

From the output distribution, the best estimates of mean, median and mode central-values can be obtained plus further statistical information, if required, such as standard deviation, skewness, kurtosis, etc. The distribution may also be presented in the form of a cumulative S-curve showing the probabilities of different outcome, represented by percentile values such as p10, p50 or p90. From these plots we may consider how confidently we may exceed threshold values that we choose to set, or establish the value against a given confidence level that we require. These outputs are discussed in the next section.

With modern computers such simulations take very little time, and, although even more structured preparation is required, the time taken to prepare a risked cash flow model can be less than the real time expended manually assessing and then interpreting the relative value of selected scenarios. For all significant investments, therefore, the advantages outweigh the apparent additional effort. Moreover, simulation capability is usually easily provided by appending additional functionality to existing spreadsheet software, although skill in applying it and in dynamic modelling must be acquired.

The time taken to prepare a risked cash flow model can be less than the real time expended manually assessing and then interpreting the relative value of selected scenarios.

Improving estimating

Without Monte Carlo simulation techniques and the use of dynamic modelling, assumptions need to be made by estimators throughout their cash flow model as to what conditions may apply and what the values of many different variables may be. Estimators might also take into account different scenarios, but there are drawbacks to this. Most scenarios are limited to changing one or two variables or making different assumptions. Other outcomes, either resulting from these variables being changed by a different amount or from other variables being changed, are not usually inspected, because to do so manually is too protracted. Equally, they do not establish the probability of any of the outcomes happening. Thus decision-makers have to trust that the single case produced by the estimators adequately approximates to the true p50 value (or whatever other value it purports to represent, e.g. mean or mode).

Both p50 and outlying values estimated by more representative Monte Carlo analyses may be substantially different from initial values established by traditional methods.

However, some risk factors will introduce very significant variability so that a very broad range of values may result. The profile of possible outcomes may also be skewed. At the same time, various estimating biases can often be introduced. Sometimes, hidden contingencies are built in by estimators to protect themselves, so that results may prove to be too pessimistic. At other times, estimates may be overtly optimistic and ignore balancing risk factors, perhaps owing to internal influences favouring a specific proposal.

It can, therefore, be very difficult to establish a reasonable central value (typically the p50 value) subjectively. Both p50 and outlying values estimated by more representative Monte Carlo analyses may be substantially different from initial values established by traditional methods. The extent of real variability and the true value of alternative possible outcomes may be more fully exposed than observed by estimating a few scenarios of 'worst' cases by trial and error. Experience shows that the differences can be significant.

Developing a model

A summary of the main stages in development and operation of a risk model is set out below.

1   Identify all assumptions and fixed value data in the model.

2   Identify all general estimating uncertainties in the model. Specify variability in terms of minimum, most likely and maximum estimates and use triangular distributions as reasonable approximations of input ranges where appropriate.

3   Map risks from a qualitative risks register and identify special risks, uncertainties or extremes. Devise conditional or probabilistic branching to represent discrete risks as necessary. Where triangular distributions do not fit, use subjective judgement or empirical historical data to define special distributions where appropriate.

4   Identify mitigation measures that would be applied if risks materialised. Design conditional modelling solutions and map to risk model.

5   Build a summary programme for critical activities with variable and conditional inputs relating to the timing of cash flows.

6   Build the model to be dynamic. Remove fixed assumptions and replace data with variable inputs and/or use formulae to build conditional inputs.

7   Identify and apply major correlations between variables.

8   Build the model in composite layers to distinguish between systemic and specific risks and to allow major sensitivities to be assessed.

9   Record and summarise the design structure of the model and all major inputs and correlations. Identify and record any risks not modelled and why.

10 Hold a team review to inspect risk mapping and risk modelling of inputs. Give special consideration to risk in each of the major elements.

11 Identify major outputs required and formats.

12 Select Monte Carlo simulation parameters and run model.

Interpreting outputs

Analysing Monte Carlo outputs

Simulations using a Monte Carlo risked cash flow model will produce ranges of results for each target output, which may be presented in different forms. By changing to a method that presents results in a different way, it is necessary to understand how to interpret them in a manner that will aid decision-making, rather than perhaps confuse decision-makers further. Because the results are presented in the form of statistical distributions, various other statistical attributes may be used to define the results. Not all of these attributes are relevant to decision-making and some are more relevant to particular decision criteria than others. The right presentations and attributes should be selected and standardised so that decision-makers become readily familiar with what is important in them. Equally, it is important to validate findings and not rely on the modelling and computer simulations to work correctly first time.

Output profiles

The first attribute to check is whether the output profiles are reasonable. The shape of each distribution should be checked to see that the simulation has produced a stable profile. If the distribution is spiked or stepped, the causes should be investigated and understood.

Additionally, the profile may be distinctly skewed because in many investment and project analyses certain inputs, which may be the major drivers, may themselves be skewed. Conversely, depending on the severity of their influences, skewness may not always show in output profiles as much as expected. Other multiple inputs, particularly if they have some correlation between them, may, when statistically combined, lead to an output profile which approximates to a normal distribution. Therefore, it is common for an output profile to be smoothed even in the face of major risks in the analysis.

Statistical values for skewness or kurtosis mean little to most decision-makers and provide no particular added value so are commonly ignored. Visual inspection of a profile commonly provides an adequate means to assess the underlying issues.

Input uncertainties are usually represented by approximations to statistical distributions. These are defined by estimating the parameters of that distribution. For example, the most commonly used distribution in uncertainty estimation is the Triangular. This is used, not only because it provides a reasonably accurate representation of many types of uncertainty, but also because its parameters (minimum, most likely and maximum) have some real meaning to those trying to come up with the estimate. Often, the minimum and maximum are replaced by optimistic and pessimistic values (representing, say, 5th and 95th percentiles) which are easier to estimate realistically than the absolute minimum and maximum.

Note, however, that you cannot simply add the minimums (maximums, or any other values except for the arithmetic means) of each distribution together to derive an equivalent minimum value for the output range, unless all input uncertainties are totally correlated. Such practice if used (and it commonly is) is generally wrong and will deliver unrealistically large spreads of possible outcomes.

Extremes

Similarly, the minimum and maximum values of the output range should be broadly validated. Because of the randomness within the simulations, repeated trials may produce different extreme values at the ends of the distributions but these will very rarely be the absolute 'worst case' minimum or maximum values possible. Unless all factors are perfectly correlated, the probability that all risks will occur together is extremely rare. Increasing the number of iterations in a simulation will theoretically extend the possible results towards the absolute worst cases, but this is unnecessary, since these absolute values are generally of little interest (since the chance of them occurring is so small). The number of iterations required is that which will produce stable output (if the simulation is repeated with different starting values for the random numbers generators) between, say, the 1st and 99th percentiles. Exactly which percentiles are required to represent adequately low and high values should be agreed before the model is run for the first time.

Central values

Interpretation of the output distributions can be more difficult than estimation of the input distributions. The resulting curves are unlikely to be totally smooth unless they can be appropriately fitted to standard statistical distributions.

A common area of confusion is which of the three common measures of centrality (i.e. some form of average) is most appropriate in telling us what we need to know. Figure 2.11 illustrates these three measures on a skewed distribution for the predicted turnover in the first year of operation of an uncertain venture. The curve represents the simulation's approximation of all possible outcomes. The area underneath the curve represents this total probability (i.e. 100 per cent).

Fig. 2.11 Interpreting central values

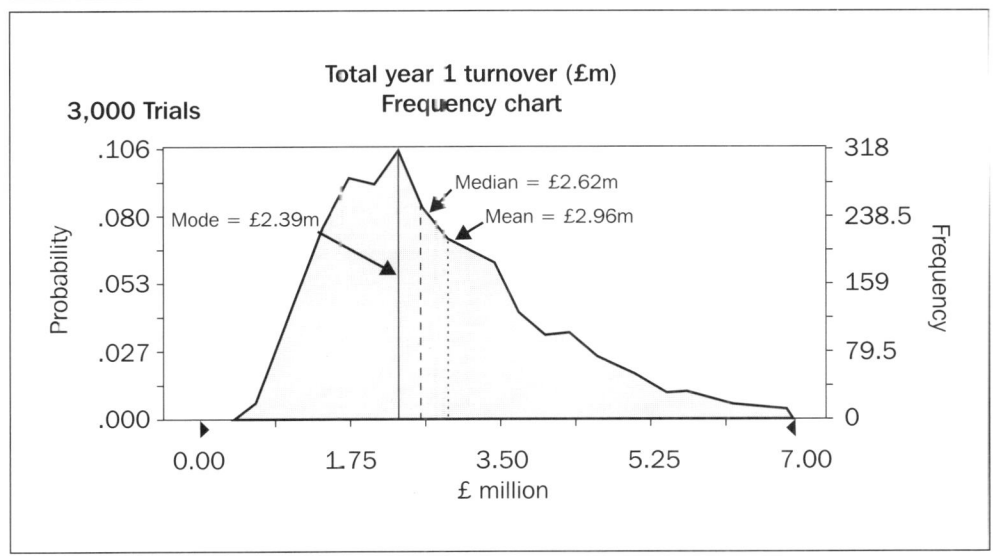

The mode, or most-likely value, is the value that occurs most frequently, and is identified as the peak of the distribution (£2.39m in the above example). In this case, there is a single peak but in some cases (especially where the resulting distribution is spiky) there may be more than one, and the mode cannot readily be calculated. It is also not necessarily very central. In this example, the likelihood of exceeding the mode is around 60 per cent. Therefore, even though the mode is often used for estimating input uncertainty (because it is easy to visualise and represents a convenient way of creating an input profile), it has limited usefulness as a measure of a central output value.

The median p50 is the value at which you have an even chance of achieving an outcome that is greater or less than that value. In the above example, 50 per cent of the curve (in terms of area) lies below £2.62m and 50 per cent above. In terms of risk, the chance of achieving or not achieving a particular target (value, date, etc.) is generally what we want the analysis to tell us. Therefore, the p50 value is probably the most widely used of the three measures.

The p50 value does not, however, tell us anything about the distribution above its 50th percentile whereas the (arithmetic) mean or expected value takes the whole distribution into account. In the above example, its value of £2.96m is significantly higher than the p50 value because of the skewness of the distribution towards the larger values. The mean is central to much statistical theory and is necessarily of prime importance where further statistical analysis of the results is required and possible. On the rare occasions when the output distributions are symmetrical (with a single peak), these central values would coincide and no distinction need be made.

Confidence levels

Distribution curves may also be presented in the form of cumulative S-curves showing the probability of the outcome exceeding or not exceeding any given value, depending on context. From these curves we may, for example, consider how confidently we may exceed threshold values that we may choose to set or establish the value we should expect to achieve against a given confidence level that we require. Figure 2.12 shows the same results achieved for year 1 turnover as shown in Figure 2.11, but in cumulative format.

From the lines added to the graph, we can see that there is a 50 per cent chance of exceeding a turnover of £2.64m (the p50 value). If it had been decided that a turnover of £3.5m is necessary to make the venture viable, we can see that there is only a 25 per cent chance of achieving or exceeding this figure.

These curves may be drawn either in ascending (as in Figure 2.12) or in descending format. Both show the same information but, as a general rule, it is best to use a descending S-curve to read off the chance that a threshold will be met or exceeded (unlike the example shown, where we have had to calculate the chance of exceeding the £3.5m threshold by subtracting the 75 per cent shown from 100 per cent). However, use an ascending curve to state the chance of not meeting a threshold.

Fig. 2.12 Cumulative probability charts

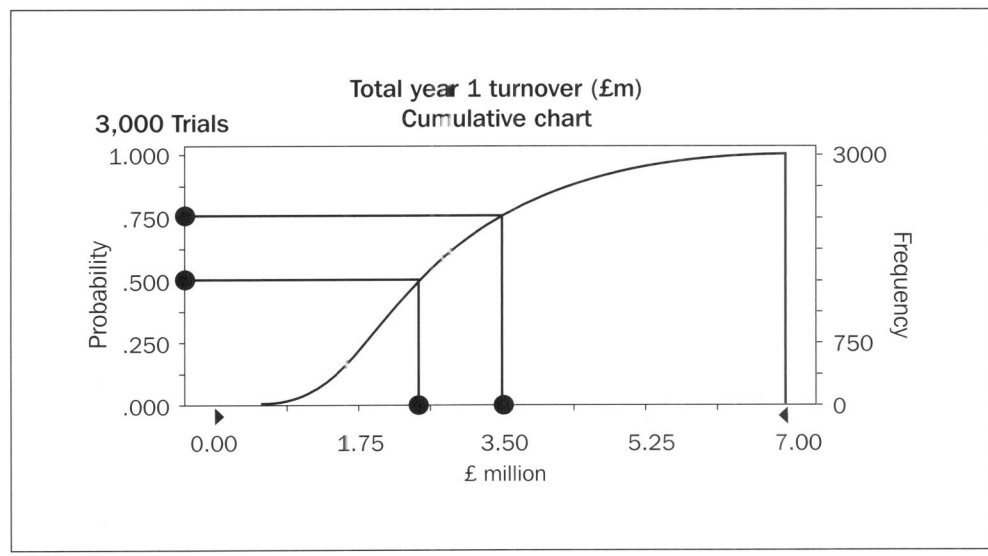

Traditional sensitivity analyses can mislead, because they do not always consider to what extent the different variables can vary.

Comparing options

Both standard distributions and S-curves are useful for comparing different investment options. Standard distributions usually give a better visual idea of the variability of different distributions but S-curves are particularly useful to show which performs best against threshold criteria.

Sensitivity analyses

Sensitivity analyses aim to show which are the main drivers behind the results so that management attention can be focused on them. Commonly, selected factors are varied by the same amount, perhaps 10 per cent, and the relative impact on outcomes are inspected.

However, traditional sensitivity analyses can mislead, because they do not always consider to what extent the different variables can vary. This is shown in the example in Figure 2.13. For the same fixed percentage change, one factor, A, may have a lower impact on the outcome than another factor, B. However, factor A may have a greater impact on the outcome in reality if it can change to a greater degree than factor B.

Fig. 2.13 Sensitivity analyses

Traditional sensitivity analysis			
A changes by fixed amount	5%	which changes outcome by	1.0%
B changes by fixed amount	5%	which changes outcome by	1.5%
B is seen to be the main driver			

Risk sensitivity analysis			
A changes to maximum possible	25%	which changes outcome by	5.0%
B changes to maximum possible	10%	which changes outcome by	3.0%
A is seen to be the risk driver			

Also, traditional sensitivity analyses cannot account for correlation between different factors, whereas this can generally be included in Monte Carlo simulations. Many software packages that provide risk simulation capability also provide the capability to conduct risk sensitivity analyses, although capabilities vary from package to package. Tornado diagrams can be produced ranking the relative effect of different issues on the outcomes. These diagrams are often demanded by decision makers, but caution should be exercised in developing and interpreting them. Different factors may represent higher or lower levels of detail than others so that comparisons may be spurious. Sensitivity analyses should therefore be layered and common criteria should be established for different prospects.

For example, the civil engineering costs of a new factory may represent only one element of the total building costs of the factory, which is one component of the capital costs of an investment which also includes operating costs. It would be inappropriate to compare the influence of this component with the influence of, say, price on demand. Instead, total costs may be compared with total revenues. After that, sub-components in either costs or revenues should be compared only with other sub-components in the same category, and so on for each level of detail.

It is also worth noting that relatively small changes to single values using normal estimating methods can produce radically different results, any of which may be selected as the supposed final estimate. In contrast, when variable estimating is used, often notable changes have to be made to the overall profiles of possible inputs before striking changes occur in the final profile of modelled outcomes or in its p50 or expected values. This observation can carry serious implications for the effectiveness of some mitigation proposals, as their effectiveness may be overrated when assessed by traditional sensitivity analyses. Effectiveness is dependent on the probability of the mitigation being achieved, which is subject to other correlating influences, which usually cannot be assessed in traditional analyses.

MANAGING RISKS AND OPPORTUNITIES – ACTIONS

Dealing with risk

The process of selecting from general categories of actions to manage opportunities and risks is worth looking at more closely as part of the planning step. For risks it resembles an incremental process of elimination. Figures 2.14 and 2.15 depict the action options and sequences involved in managing risk.

The cost consequences of failing even to identify an uncertainty with major risk implications can be:

- non-existent, if the risk fails to materialise;
- dire if it does and management is caught having to react to it by improvising in the absence of planning and preparation.

Responding to risks demands a structured consideration of what is possible, effective and cost-efficient.

> Responding to risks demands a structured consideration of what is possible, effective and cost-efficient.

Fig. 2.14 Risk management choices

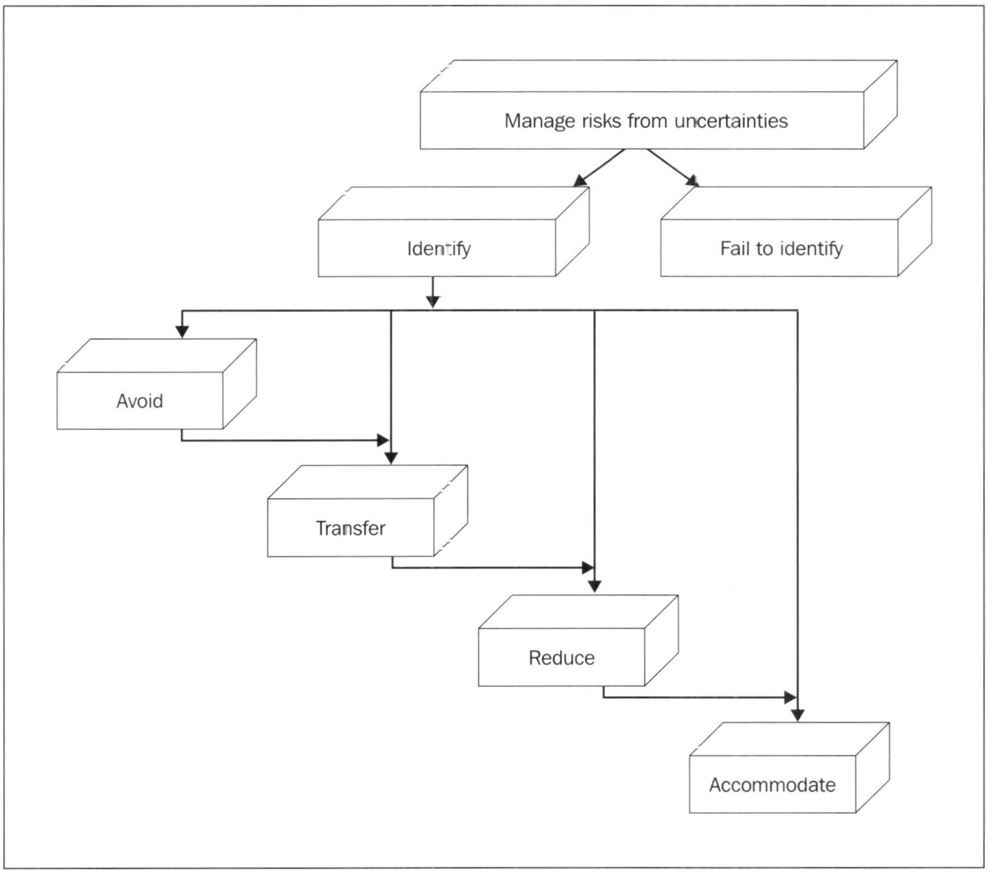

Assuming it is identified, Figure 2.14 shows the progressive whittling away of the influence of adverse risks through:

- avoidance
- transfer
- reduction
- accommodation.

Avoidance

This first possibility is exactly what the word implies. For example, abandonment of an untried technology avoids the associated technical risk. Carrying out work in environmentally protected facilities to avoid weather impacts and pursuing a policy against partnering with government-controlled enterprises in specific countries are other examples.

Transfer

Where options for avoidance either do not exist, are unacceptable or are only partially effective, transfer can be considered as an alternative or as a means of further shifting the risk burden. This entails transferring of ownership of the consequences of risk and is typically effected through contractual mechanisms. Insurance represents a specific form of total or partial transfer. Risk-sharing, usually linked with some gain-sharing arrangement, is yet another method of partial transfer.

Reduction

What cannot be, or is best not, avoided or transferred remains and must be dealt with directly by measures to reduce it. Figure 2.15 further breaks down the components of risk reduction.

- *Prevention* amounts to reducing the likelihood of adverse events or circumstances.
- *Mitigation* works at lessening the impacts of adversity where it is not successfully prevented and, consequently, materialises.
- *Containment* measures seek to ensure that what remains of the risk after efforts to prevent and mitigate is limited either by active intervention or by contractual arrangements such as 'capping' of liabilities.

Fig. 2.15 Risk reduction

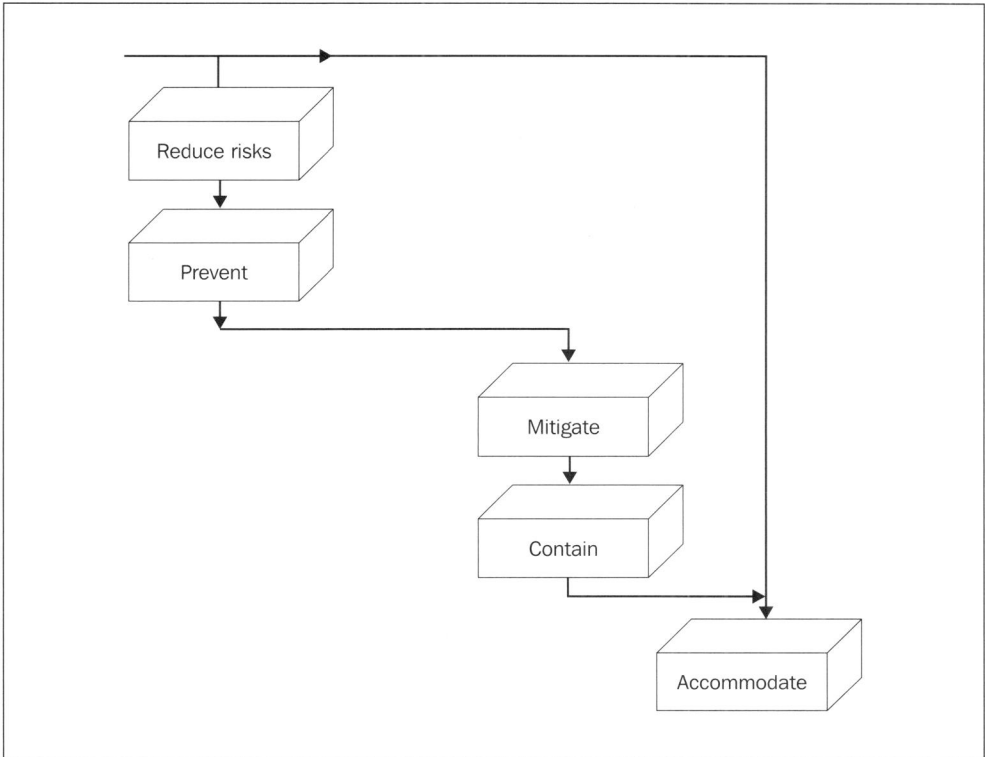

All agreed uncertainty management actions to be incorporated in baseline plans should also be costed and budgeted to justify them and to provide adequate funding.

However, fall back and contingency measures are often treated separately from other mitigation measures where they are not included in baseline plans and budgets. These are exemplified by the disaster recovery plan which sits on the shelf, only to be activated on the occurrence of predefined conditions. Its budgetary provisions must be sought elsewhere if not accommodated within specific investment-related budgets.

Accommodation

After all options to minimise the influence of risk have been considered and exercised as appropriate, what is left can only be accommodated by strategies which offer sufficient margin, flexibility or resilience to withstand the possible consequences without catastrophic results.

Opportunities – more easily managed, more frequently forgotten

For managing opportunities, Figure 2.16 illustrates a much more straightforward sequence. Failure to identify an uncertainty giving rise to major opportunity can lead to:

- no loss if the opportunity never materialises;
- significant lost reward if it does materialise and is missed;
- significant diminution of potential reward if it materialises and management has to react without adequate planning and preparation.

Fig. 2.16 The opportunity management sequence

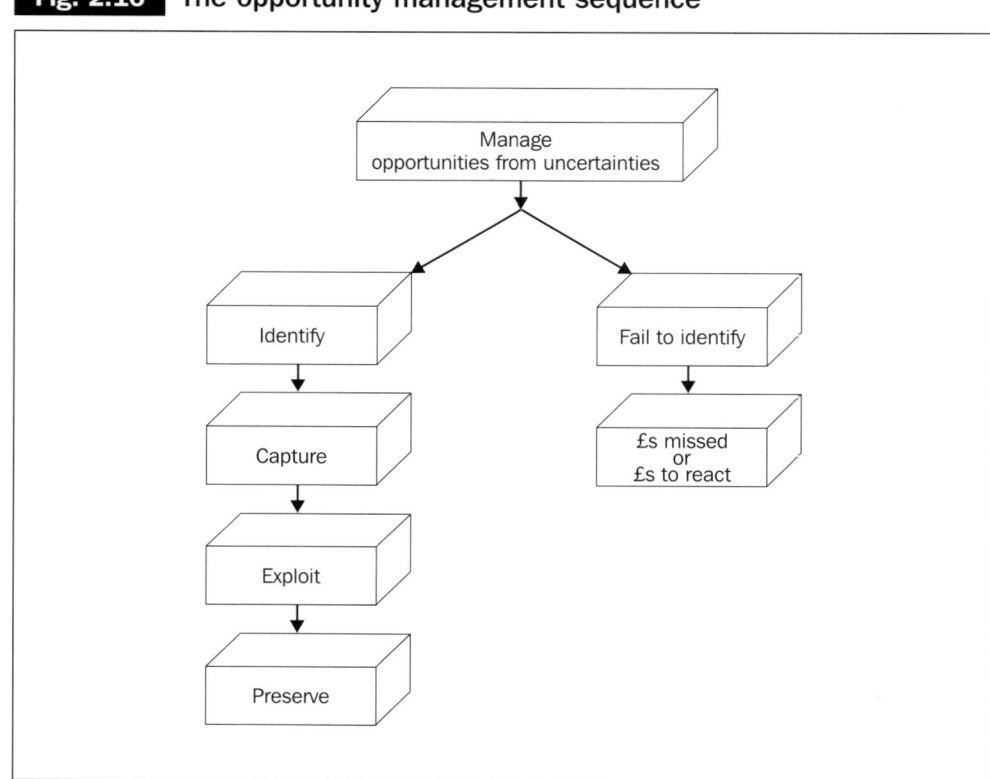

Assuming the opportunity is identified, the management actions are capture, exploit and preserve.

Capture

The basic principle of being in the right place at the right time exemplifies the measures designed to capture. In strategic marketing this amounts to positioning to exploit identified market opportunity. For the individual investment, contractual options and other forms of hedging are means of ensuring ability to take advantage of fortuitous circumstances should they arise.

Exploit

The counterpart of risk mitigation, exploitation is simply the maximising and realisation of the potential offered by opportunities. Like mitigation action, any measure designed to exploit usually pays great dividends in return for planning and preparation. Unfortunately, where investors become preoccupied with risk, preparations for exploiting opportunity tend either to take a back seat or be totally forgotten.

Preserve

Having implemented strategies and taken any initial actions to successfully derive reward from opportunity, it may still be necessary to actively safeguard the reward potential. Particularly where derivation of reward occurs over an extended period (e.g. during the operational life of an asset), remaining 'ahead of the game' might make the difference between realisation of full reward potential and delivered benefits which fall far short of what could have been. During the operation stage, ongoing proactive uncertainty management itself may become the primary preservation measure.

Managing the exceptional/liabilities

There are two categories of investment risk which represent exceptional liabilities for the business:

- legal responsibilities;
- catastrophes.

> The existence and extent of legal responsibilities and potential liabilities should always be 'flagged' in the grading and prioritising of risks and management actions in the uncertainty register.

Legal responsibilities

What makes legal responsibilities exceptional is the extent of exposure that business management can be left to accommodate after taking what might seem to be all reasonable measures to prevent and mitigate liabilities arising under law.

- Laws, particularly those involving public health and safety and the environment, are subject to change.
- Although ultimately influenced by the principle of reasonable conduct, legal liabilities arise automatically on the occurrence of prescribed events or circumstances, and can lead to fixed penalties or virtually unlimited damages.

The existence and extent of legal responsibilities and potential liabilities should always be 'flagged' in the grading and prioritising of risks and management actions in the uncertainty register.

The tobacco industry offers a sobering example where changing social attitudes and emergent legal precedents have led to a redefinition of legal responsibilities and liabilities.

Catastrophes

Catastrophes are exceptional by virtue of the scale of adverse consequences or impacts. They are not always the extremely low-probability disasters or acts of God. Where the catastrophe is avoidable and also involves failure to meet legal responsibilities, the consequences to a company may be both socially devastating and financially crippling.

Disaster recovery has blossomed as a specialised management field where contingency planning is highly developed to cater for the would-be catastrophe. The whole emphasis is on mitigation of the unprevented or unpreventable. It is *not* a substitute for the preventive elements of risk management.

Management procedures for catastrophic risk should ensure that the exceptional consequence risk gets the exceptional management attention it warrants. It can be singled out in the risk scoring system for the uncertainty register with a particularly high score reserved for such risks. Planning and quantitative analysis activities can use scenario modelling to develop detailed solutions. The extent of management commitment necessary to adequately address catastrophic risk may well warrant its being budgeted as a separate item at the business level.

CHAPTER REVIEW

- Entrepreneurial energy and enterprise need to be harnessed in pursuit of the achievable, through structured, transparent and accountable management of uncertainty, risk and opportunity.

- Effective management of uncertainty must recognise the possible undesirable or limiting influences of objective data based on experience and of suspect assumptions considered immune to challenge.

- As uncertainty management can deal only with identified uncertainties, priority effort needs to be directed at discovering uncertainties that give rise to significant risk and opportunity.

- Broad participation in the uncertainty management process is the best guarantee of common focus and coordinated effort by those affecting, affected by or carrying out investment related work.

- There is no substitute for quantitative analysis of uncertainties in support of dimensional decisions where cost/benefit trade-offs prevail.

- Management of investment and business uncertainty needs to shed the 'downside' mindset which is the legacy of risk management if it is to capture and exploit opportunities that surpass expectations.
- The potential for legal responsibilities and catastrophes to impact on investment and business performance argues for their exceptional treatment within the uncertainty management process.

Part Two

Stages

Stage 1: Developing a strategy

INTRODUCTION

It is essential for a company to develop a strategy to capitalise on its opportunities and strengths while minimising its weaknesses and exposure to risks. Therefore, clear evaluation of the risks by the whole business is essential to the selection of a good strategy but, equally, understanding by the business of the goals, risks and management of those risks is essential to delivering the strategy and achieving the best realisable value.

In this chapter, we discuss the basic steps, methodologies and analyses necessary to formulate a strategy, but equal emphasis is given to extracting strategic information from the analyses in order to pursue it through the selection, appraisal and management of appropriate investments. Issues discussed, therefore, focus on the additional role of strategic analysis as preparatory work to permit clear and logical decision-making to be subsequently applied. Detailed methodologies for developing strategies are beyond the scope of the present book.

The major topics covered are as follows:

■ *Strategic objectives*   Distinctions between product, business unit and corporate objectives, also generic strategies, their applicability and expectations.

■ *Defining the business environment*   The major factors affecting strategies and recommended analyses to summarise them.

■ *Forecasting the future*   Techniques to identify future opportunities and risks using scenario analyses, also the use of decision trees and systems dynamics modelling to validate scenarios and strategic options.

■ *Developing a portfolio*   Sources of opportunity and risks and strategic objectives for a portfolio, including growth, maintenance, diversification and risk-limiting policy.

> It is essential for a company to develop a strategy to capitalise on its opportunities and strengths while minimising its weaknesses and exposure to risks.

DEVELOP STRATEGIC OBJECTIVES

Define strategy

There are many aspects to a strategy, including differences between product/market, business unit and corporate strategies as indicated in Figure 3.1. Strategy generally refers to the major decisions that a business must make about where it is heading and how (in principle) it intends to get there. It need not refer to specific investments, although key 'strategic' investments may form an integral part of a strategy. Similarly, business plans may be confused with strategy, but they are usually specific tactical proposals to deliver strategic aims.

Fig. 3.1 Hierarchy of strategies and portfolios

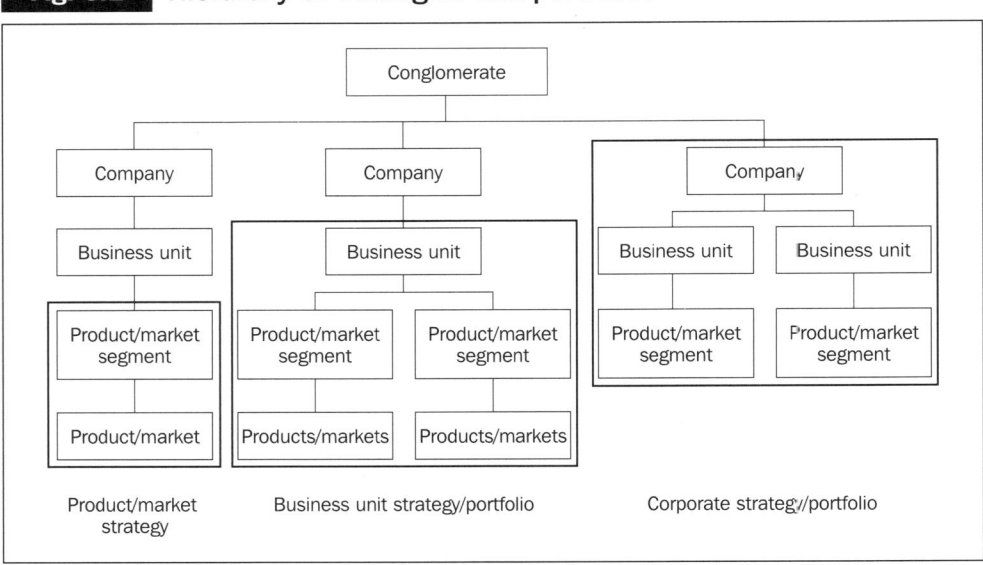

Develop product/market strategies

The first strategic issues a business unit needs to define are: what product or service it is trying to sell, why there is a market for it, and how it will present its product and compete in the marketplace. Its strategy is likely to follow one of the following generic forms:

■ cost leader;

■ focused player;

■ quality leader;

■ specialised niche player;

■ differentiated by marketing;

■ brand leader;

■ differentiated by innovation.

What form of strategy is appropriate may depend largely on the structure and power of the market and the industry forces. In some industries, external forces and risks may be very strong and strategic choice may be reduced.

Align the business unit

A strategy can also be defined by the composition of internal strengths and weaknesses such as:

■ skills and resources;

■ structure of the company and processes;

- culture and attitudes;

- financing arrangements.

In contrast to external forces, internal factors are considered more controllable and may be changed if necessary. Often, to ensure that the internal factors align with the preferred market strategy, a business may embark on a major change-management programme to realign the business.

Sometimes a change programme itself is described as a strategy but this loses sight of the objective. A change programme is essentially a project to deliver the means to pursue a business strategy. Such changes themselves frequently involve major investments and are subject to considerable risks. Change programmes should, therefore, be assessed both in terms of their strategic fit and their own risks and rewards. They should be evaluated through all the phases of the framework discussed in this book as if they were normal capital investment projects.

Develop business unit and corporate strategies

A company acquires a portfolio as soon as it develops more than one distinct product or market, which it generally does for one of the following principal reasons:

- maintenance of the portfolio;

- growth to pursue specific opportunities;

- diversification to reduce risk;

- strategic growth to generally improve opportunity or reduce costs or risks.

Growing sales to increase total profit is often the first reason for adding products or businesses to a portfolio. New products may also be introduced simply to maintain the portfolio, by replacing existing products over time if demand or competition are adversely affecting sales of the older products. Alternatively, new products may be introduced just to offset variability in revenue from existing products. This diversifies risk and smooths cash flows and revenues. Another reason for pursuing growth is to manage strategic risk and opportunity by seeking to limit competition and dominate a market. Alternatively, the business may divest itself of products or markets that are performing poorly.

However, new products may transfer risk to or reduce reward from existing products. Even when products support each other, priorities invariably need to be set to prioritise resource allocations between them. To various degrees, different products and markets may be considered to compete with each other.

Acquiring or divesting products or entering or withdrawing from markets complicates both the analysis and the management of a business. It is not a matter of simply looking at the benefits of the one product. A business unit strategy is required to balance and maintain an optimum portfolio. Individual investments should be assessed against both the needs of the portfolio and the underlying product strategy.

When the portfolio becomes large, it is likely that products and markets will be grouped into individual business units. Greater value can be derived if synergies can be found through a corporate strategy that does not impose excessive trade-offs between the individual business unit strategies. The role of corporate management is to find the right mix of strategic investments or businesses and develop a corporate structure to deliver optimal rewards.

DEFINE THE BUSINESS ENVIRONMENT

Individual investments should be assessed against both the needs of the portfolio and the underlying product strategy.

Identify major factors

An early aim of strategic analysis is to identify the major factors that must be balanced to optimise the potential rewards to the company. Although specific factors are unique to every company, generic categories include:

- nature of products or services, technologies and skills;
- market demand and pricing structures;
- competitive environment and attitudes;
- suppliers and cost structure;
- economic factors;
- regulatory and legal environment;
- social and political environment;
- corporate strengths and weaknesses;
- attitudes to risk and reward;
- relationships with financial markets/lenders;
- business cycle and speed of changes.

Analyse major issues

Key techniques commonly used to identify and analyse the factors are as follows:

- *Establish a baseline* – size of the industry, company, number of competitors, etc.
- *Segment the market* and position your company and competitors.
- *Establish a view* of the value-chain and key drivers.

- *Conduct a SWOT* (Strengths/Weaknesses/Opportunities/Threats) *analysis* for your company and a competitor analysis for comparison.

- *Identify other external drivers* such as those indicated by Michael Porter, e.g. 'five forces' (buyers/suppliers/competitors/substitutes/corporate), and by PEST (political/economic/social/technical) analyses.

- *Define* the industry/business cycle.

These basic analyses capture and present information in a manner useful for developing a strategy. No single analytical technique should be expected to give a solution. Instead, applying multiple techniques ensures that all major factors have been identified and are understood. It is important that the process is planned: over-analysis will lead to 'analysis paralysis' whereas oversimplification of important factors and relationships will give a false sense of security and hide potential risks.

In particular, the SWOT and PEST analyses provide very useful summaries of major risks and opportunities. Their method of information capture is especially practical when later screening or fully appraising specific investments. As shown in Figure 3.2, the issues should be prioritised by scoring and ranking them.

> No single analytical technique should be expected to give a solution

Fig. 3.2 Ranked SWOT analysis

Strengths (Internal)	Score	Weaknesses (Internal)	Score
New product in pipeline	5	Poor coordinated planning	6
Total solution supplier	5	Width of product range	4
System building capacity	4	Sales vs marketing led	4
Skilled workforce	4	Poor performance in USA	3
Experience of China market	3	Size of company	2
CE mark quality	3		

Opportunities (External)	Score	Threats (External)	Score
Demand for analytical solutions	5	Wildly fluctuating demand	6
Major competitor in management buy-out	4	Third-world suppliers	4
Upgrade/refit work	3	Chaos in developing countries	3
Standards may favour our technology	3	Vertical integration of suppliers	3
Shift from h/w to s/w solutions	3	Move from big to small systems	2
Single source agreements	2	Environmental health concerns	2
		Standards may not favour our technology	2

Developing scenarios is a process that should give full recognition to uncertainty, including changes in the environment, imperfect knowledge and (even) irrational behaviour.

Various strategic analysis software packages are available to aid this information exploration and analysis phase. Such software not only seeks to ask questions and process the data, but it provides a single focal point to ensure that the right questions are asked and assessed. Such packages discourage an *ad hoc* approach and possibly prevent a hard-pressed analyst overlooking critical factors that may be essential in later analyses or presenting incomplete and thereby misleading views. However, packages vary in the extent of analysis they provide and all analyses must be tailored to needs.

ENVISAGE THE FUTURE

Identify strategic scenarios

The strategic analyses mentioned so far are useful in defining separate issues such as how a business and its competitors are positioned in the market, where they have been and where they might be going. Consideration of alternative scenarios should identify where major strategic opportunities and risks exist, how they may be brought about and what their likelihood of occurrence could be. Brainstorming sessions should creatively identify possible future developments and opportunities in the business environment by addressing what may happen if key factors or drivers identified in the intitial strategic analyses are changed. The recording of assumptions, risks or challenges to perceived logic in a summary register, as the scenario analysis proceeds, allows these issues to be reviewed at a future time when screening or appraising specific investments. Otherwise, outcomes which may appear obvious with hindsight may be overlooked in later periods of a venture.

It is unreasonable to expect to be able to predict *all* outcomes and it is wise to keep a high-level perspective on the likelihood and impact of different strategic approaches.

Developing scenarios is a process that should give full recognition to uncertainty, including changes in the environment, imperfect knowledge and (even) irrational behaviour. In the modern competitive business environment, the status quo is rarely maintained for long. Potential step-changes to how the industry operates may be identified and these changes may either pose a serious risk or provide a strategic opportunity depending on the business's own strengths and weaknesses. Historical experience can discourage the development of scenarios but very often, by temporarily ignoring constraints, the consequences reached may themselves indicate how an unexpected change could logically occur.

However, the extent of effort put into scenario generation needs to be controlled. It is unreasonable to expect to be able to predict *all* outcomes and it is wise to keep a high-level perspective on the likelihood and impact of different strategic approaches. Too many scenarios within scenarios can be confusing.

Analyse strategic scenarios

Different strategic options and views of the future are captured by constructing decision trees to model the consequences and possible reactions to different outcomes. The branches of such decision trees will map key relationships where each branch from a node will represent different possible outcomes. A major advantage of using decision trees is that scenarios can be quickly investigated and both the most likely outcome and the net value of a range of scenarios can be determined. Decision trees distinguish between choices and uncertainties and reduce multiple scenarios to a few select options.

Modern software packages are now available which can rapidly draw, edit and present diagrams of the important relationships They can include diverse factors and can incorporate uncertainties with the inputs. Many scenarios and variable factors within a proposed strategy can be modelled together by the use of systems dynamics modelling incorporating Monte Carlo analysis. They are sufficiently flexible to allow the potential variability of multiple scenarios identified previously in decision tree analyses to be re-modelled together easily and ranges of possible output values to be determined.

Alternatively, spreadsheet models can be developed with similar analytical functionality and they provide the advantage of a familiar tool set to many analysts, but they also diminish the accessibility that a graphical model and presentation provides for a senior audience. Commonly, either type of model can easily become unwieldy if too much complexity is built in or hidden within the model. Whichever form is adopted, significant benefit can be derived directly from the focused thought required to build a model of the business.

> Significant benefit can be derived directly from the focused thought required to build a model of the business.

DEVELOP A PORTFOLIO

Identify opportunities and risks

To develop and optimise a portfolio, opportunities in the business environment are matched with the objectives for both growth and maintenance of the portfolio and management of strategic risks. Opportunities will take one of the following forms:

- acquisitions;
- mergers;
- market developments;
- internal new product/service developments;

- internal product/service extensions;
- cost-cutting programmes;
- divestments.

Each of these forms is itself likely to present a different level of strategic risk to the company. Internal strategic strengths and weaknesses are very relevant. For example, if the business strategy is based primarily on product innovation, the company is likely to have strengths in this field and be better placed to manage potentially high risks associated with internal new product/service development. If opportunities do not exist internally, the second option may be to acquire or merge with another business, provided that the other business possesses innovative strengths. Acquisitions or mergers usually involve expensive and risky change-management programmes and the risks must be offset against the potential rewards. Some businesses may not possess the requisite strengths to manage the transition, to control costs and to capitalise on synergies.

Plan product portfolio growth and maintenance

Another picture of potential portfolio risk is demonstrated by the traditional product/market matrix view shown in Figure 3.3. The matrix presents four different options based on developing existing or new products in existing or new markets.

Fig. 3.3 Product/market development risk matrix

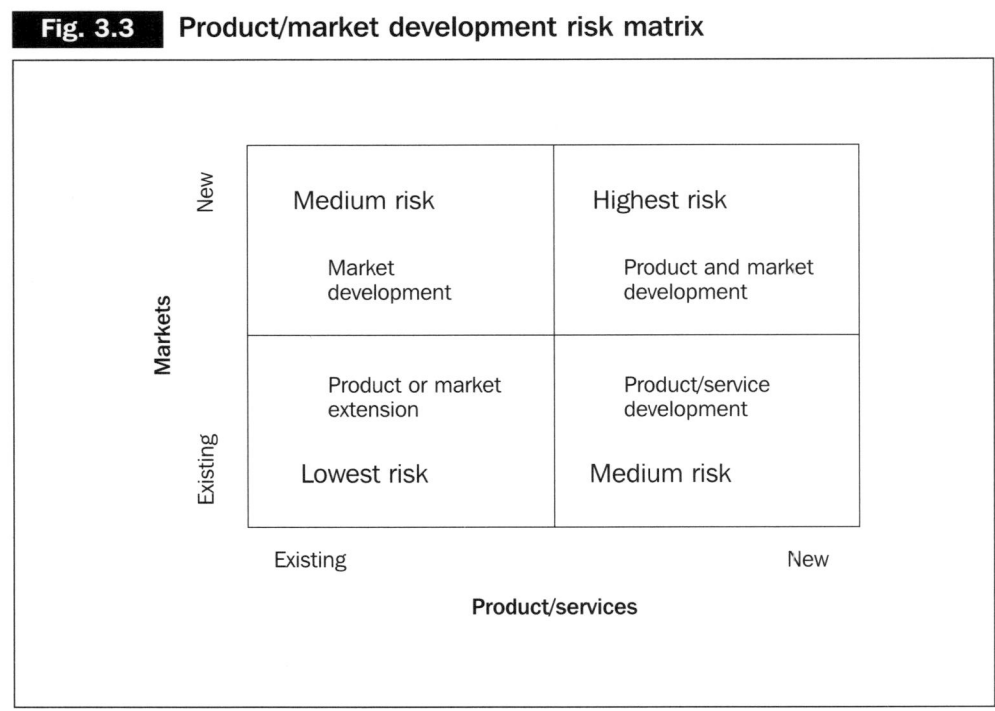

Generically, the highest overall risk is from developing new products in new markets because uncertainties and risks from both sources are compounded. Such opportunities may be considered strategically undesirable for a major proportion of the portfolio. One of the middle-ranking options may be preferred because the business possesses strategic strengths in either product development or marketing. If new products and/or markets are pursued which are similar, the business may benefit overall from direct capital and resource efficiencies or synergies between product and resource attributes, which may enhance their combined value. Synergies may be found in various areas including shared costs or marketing which may either reduce net costs or increase net revenues.

Development of existing types of products in existing markets is generally considered the least risky option, although rewards may be low and may not fulfil growth objectives. This form of development might take the form of ongoing internal product/service extensions for existing customers. However, even simple expansion plans are not risk free and introducing new products may not guarantee better rewards, even when they are closely aligned with existing business factors. There are always new uncertainties or risks when altering products or services. New options may introduce other significant risks such as possible quality issues if expansion is carried out too hastily. New products can damage profitable markets for existing products. Many corporate development strategies (e.g. some IT infrastructure developments) that are intended to improve performance or create synergies may actually involve very high-risk projects. Assessing them more carefully for risk and reward will reduce the potential for critical damage to the major operating functions in the business.

Because the business environment constantly changes, the business must also often find sources of new products and markets simply to maintain an existing portfolio. A useful picture of how to view and set objectives for maintaining a product portfolio and how to approach risks within the portfolio is provided by the matrix in Figure 3.4. This matrix is based on the classic Boston Box approach advanced by the Boston Consulting Group and the Directional Policy Matrix advanced by the McKinsey Consulting firm, which suggest that businesses possess four types of projects in a portfolio at any point in time – 'dogs', 'cash cows', 'stars' and 'question marks'. This view is particularly useful for fast-moving consumer goods (FMCG) companies but the principles apply to other industries. Use of the matrix will highlight gaps and imbalances in the business portfolio and will suggest strategic responses to risks presented by particular investments.

Current major revenue is provided by 'cash cows' but businesses may also possess 'dogs' which it may be appropriate to dispose of at the right time owing to poor performance. In the medium term, future revenue will be provided by the 'stars' and some new investment will be required to bring them forward, whilst

Many corporate development strategies that are intended to improve performance or create synergies may actually involve very high-risk projects.

for longer-term growth, some exploratory investment in opportunities denoted as 'question marks' will also be required.

Fig. 3.4 View of portfolio development and generic risk responses

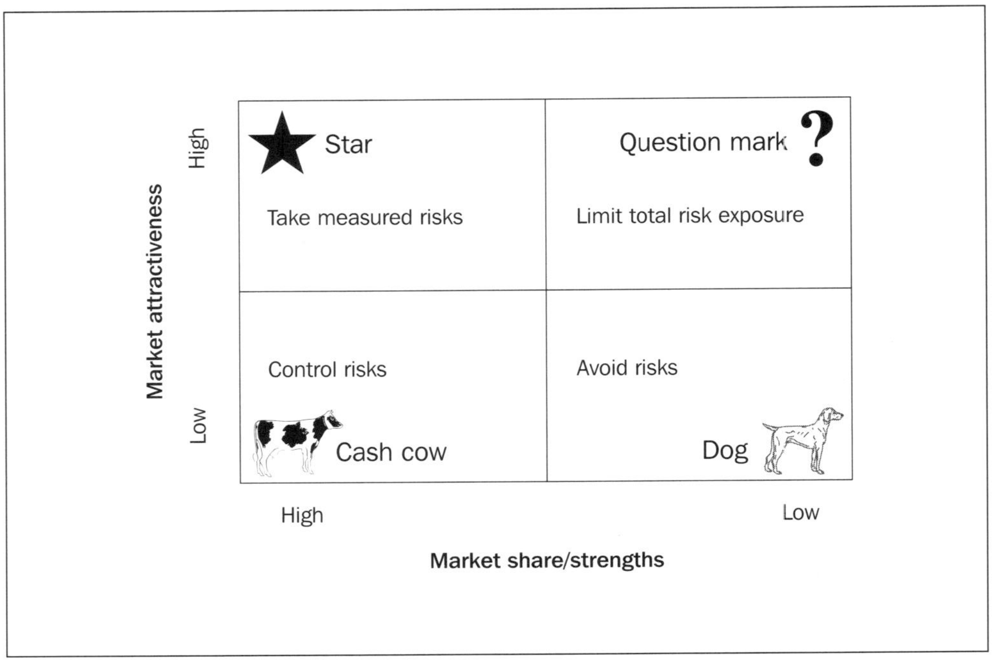

The total investment in 'question marks' may be quite significant if the company pursues an innovative strategy as occurs in an R&D based organisation. Their success may be based not just on innovation but on effective early screening of opportunities and strict control of research costs which may quickly be cut if prospects do not develop. Here, risk is usually diversified among a number of separate opportunities, whereas for businesses with few such opportunities, major investment would be riskier. Otherwise, strategies for major investment to sustain a portfolio should generally fall between 'stars' and possible reinvestment in 'cash cows'. Expansion or product enhancement programmes are examples. Major new investment should not generally be put into 'dogs', which should be managed for lowest costs.

Businesses should consciously determine what limits they notionally should set for the levels of risk they can tolerate across a portfolio

Define risk limits

As businesses develop their portfolios, some ventures will be riskier than others and the total risk to the portfolio increases as the relative share of higher risk ventures in the portfolio increases. Businesses should consciously determine what limits they notionally should set for the levels of risk they can tolerate across a portfolio, although ideal opportunities within these constraints may not actually present themselves.

There are many good reasons why a business might want to limit the level of risks it accepts. For example, high-risk venture companies, once established, may only wish to maintain sustainable revenue or growth, and further high-risk opportunities may not fit with their strengths. New products with lower risk and possibly lower returns may be introduced simply to offset variability in revenue from existing products and smooth cash flows. This may enable them to fund development to capture future rewards from other higher risk ventures. Businesses must sometimes ride out bad periods in order to be able to capitalise on better times and they may need to work with longer and less flexible time-scales than investors who can switch quickly if they choose to. The result might be to limit the pursuit of investments with relatively high risk levels to a percentage of the total portfolio, as shown in Figure 3.5.

 **Fig. 3.5** Portfolio risk levels

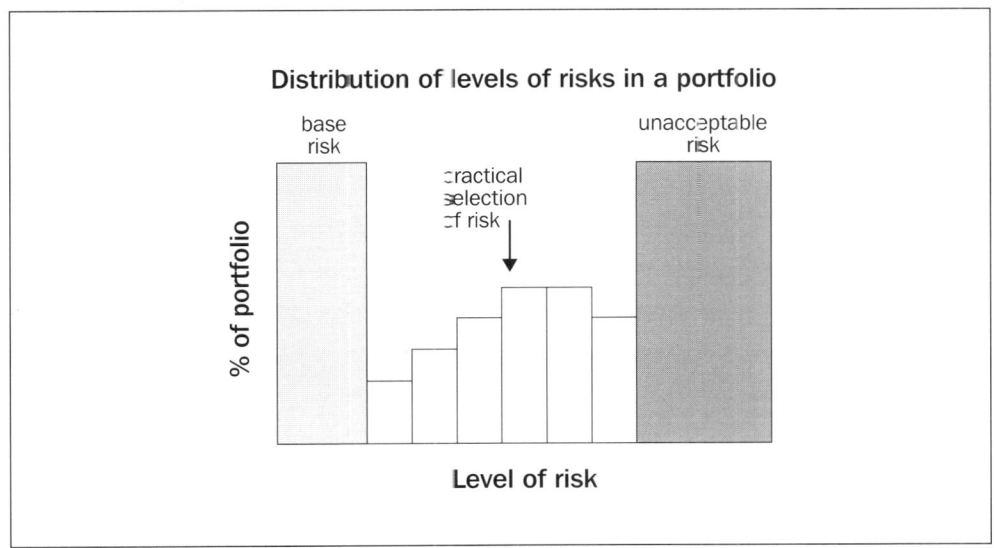

Categories and limits for key risk factors and establishing a methodology to derive qualitative scores of risk levels for different ventures relative to a portfolio are discussed in Chapter 4. Chapter 5 shows how risk levels may also be quantitatively measured by the use of risk modelling techniques.

Optimising a portfolio

Market investment theories on risk versus reward lead to the concept of a 'frontier' for investments. The frontier is a line representing a range of optimal investments with different risk and reward trade-offs, as shown in Figure 3.6. In each case, an investment on the frontier offers the maximum reward for a given level of risk or offers the minimum risk for a given reward level from among the available choices of investments.

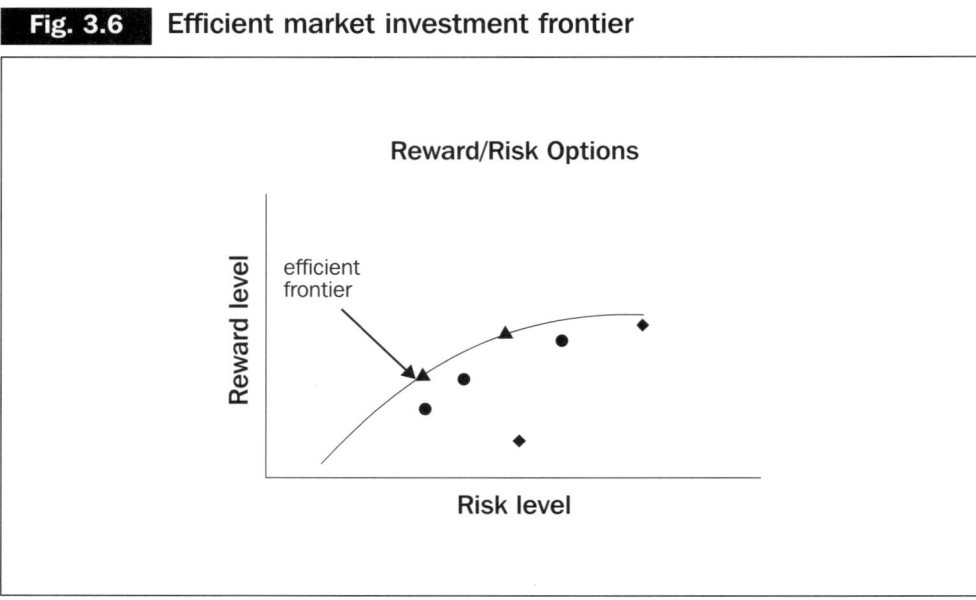

Fig. 3.6 Efficient market investment frontier

Diversification
may encourage
over-reliance by
businesses on risk
management through
statistical means,
which may undermine
businesses'
responsibility for
active management
of risks.

This suggests that the value of a portfolio will be optimised if it contains only those investments that lie close to the frontier. However, further work by Markowitz and others contends that there is an 'efficient frontier' where specific risk has been largely diversified away. Specific risks are 'unique' to each investment whereas systemic risks apply to all investments, which cannot be diversified away because they are correlated.

Some of this theory appears to be supported by empirical observation and may be applied in principle to how businesses assess their investments and portfolios. However, as with many theories, certain simplifying assumptions are made. One generalised assumption is that investors have a limitless number of investments to choose from. Another is that the options within a portfolio are presumed to be uncorrelated and investors hold only small quantities of shares in any business as part of their own fully diversified portfolios.

Businesses do not have a limitless source of opportunities. They may need to choose among finite options, their options may be highly correlated and some will dominate a portfolio so that specific risk is not diversified. Moreover, at an individual business level, companies are likely to consider pursuing similar investments because of their strengths in particular fields and investors would expect them to do so.

In contrast, conglomerates with noticeably different businesses can diversify, but many economists question why businesses should do this when the investors can do this for themselves. Furthermore, diversification may encourage over-reliance by businesses on risk management through statistical means, which may undermine businesses' responsibility for active management of risks.

Fig. 3.7 Attractive business investment frontier and risk/reward envelope

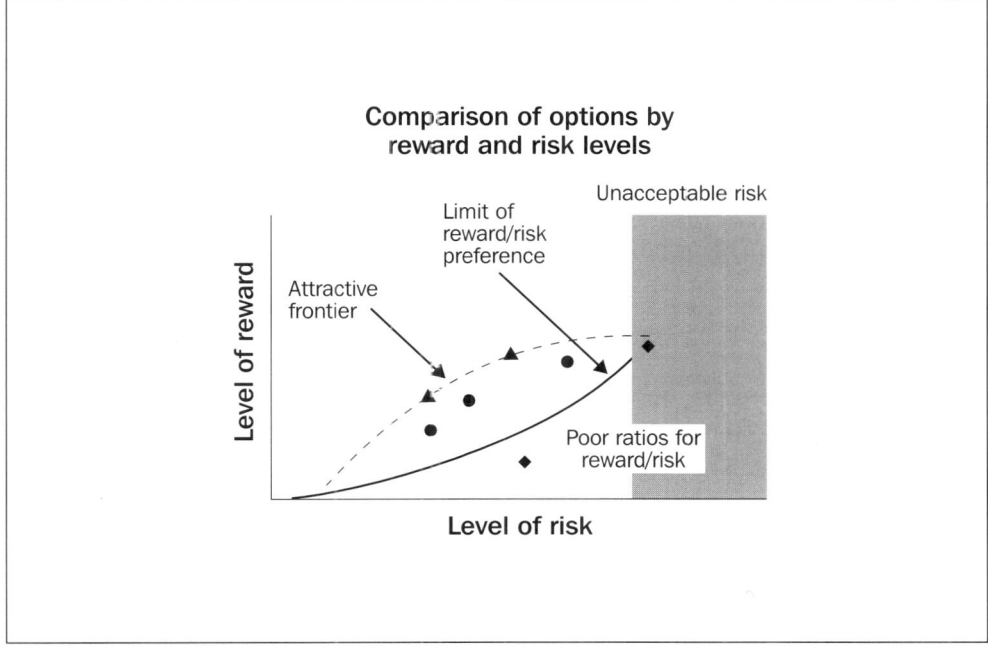

Comparison of options by reward and risk levels

Businesses can develop an envelope of 'attractive' risk and reward options.

Considering practical constraints on limiting risk levels, it is improbable that all options pursued by businesses will lie on an 'efficient' frontier as recommended by market investment theories. However, businesses can develop an envelope of 'attractive' risk and reward options as shown in Figure 3.7. Techniques to score options according to risk and reward are demonstrated in Chapter 4.

Diversification and synergies

A strategy may require that ventures are sought that carry unrelated risks so that the extent of total risk in the portfolio is diversified directly by the lack of correlation between them, or investments may be selected that are inversely correlated with each other so that specific risk is cancelled out. However, diversification presents a dilemma.

An industry's systemic risks cannot be diversified. Oil companies cannot avoid risk from changes in oil price affecting all their investments. If they seek to diversify their systemic risk, they must venture into new businesses largely unaffected by oil. Various businesses have taken such actions before but the logic is often questionable because outcomes in business are dependent on internal strengths as much as external risk. If businesses fully diversify then they can fail to take advantage of internal strengths and little value is added. Some conglomerates believe that they can offer common advantages through synergies based on efficient corporate centres, financing and management styles, but evidence suggests that all strategies based primarily on synergies should be challenged and rigorously assessed for how real the supposed benefits may be. Even within individual businesses, trade-offs against separate product strategies may outweigh the supposed additional benefits from synergies.

Nevertheless, some diversification in a portfolio is both inevitable owing to real specific risks and some is likely to be desirable to reduce total risk exposure. It is the degree of diversification and reasons for it that matter, not the principle.

Justify size

Growth, particularly through mergers and acquisitions, may be pursued as a strategy to reduce risks and increase opportunity by dominating the market through increased size and market share. To what extent this is advisable or fruitful will depend on the strength of external forces and on how well the companies can be integrated. Mergers or acquisitions may simply increase the size of the combined companies without increasing net value, although they may protect erosion of value by competitive forces. Size can bring economies of scale, but size can also increase complexities and the law of diminishing returns can easily apply.

CHAPTER REVIEW

- This chapter has demonstrated that businesses must develop strategies at product, business unit and corporate levels. Product strategies principally define the approach required to develop a business, consistent with single product/market needs and corporate abilities in that area. Business unit and corporate strategies, on the other hand, are aimed at developing a portfolio of products or companies to balance opportunities and risks in a broader landscape.

- To develop a strategy, identify all major influencing factors and support evaluation and discovery by a proper exploration of the major uncertainties and risks through the appropriate use of scenario analyses. A summary of key analyses has been provided to aid discovery, exploration and prioritisation of the issues in logical sequence, including decision trees and systems dynamic modelling to evaluate scenarios and risks.

- Corporate businesses may need their strategic investments to satisfy various objectives, from simple maintenance of a portfolio within a business unit to management of strategic risks and opportunities, depending on the balance of power of external forces and internal strengths. Strategists should be sceptical of simplistic reasons for diversification or synergies and of the likelihood of delivery of perceived benefits.

■ When the nature and substance of a chosen strategy is communicated to the business, it is equally important that the nature of the underlying opportunities and risks are also communicated. Make information from the strategic analyses available to those involved in the selection, appraisal and management of strategic investment options. In particular, record strategic assumptions, uncertainties and risks in a suitable manner such as a register and communicate information from strategic SWOT analyses. This information is used in the following chapters.

4

Stage 2: Screening investment opportunities

INTRODUCTION

In this chapter we discuss the need to create and screen investment opportunities and describe the methodologies and procedures to do so. The main topics covered are as follows:

- *Creating opportunities* Approaches to creating opportunities and the need to focus creativity and screen options.

- *Defining the options* The nature and source of information to define options for screening, including the use of cost/benefit/risk registers to summarise information.

- *Designing the screening process* Principal criteria to apply when screening and procedures and responsibilities to manage the process.

- *Eliminating and comparing options* Techniques including value preference modelling to eliminate options and to compare options against each other and against the portfolio.

- *Managing and communicating* Involvement of senior management and responsibilities for an effective process.

The more options that a company creates the better chance it will have of finding one that will deliver real value.

CREATE OPPORTUNITIES

Use creative approaches

Sometimes a strategic review will identify specific investment opportunities, which may themselves even determine the strategy. However, many investment opportunities arise at different times and come from diverse sources. Research and development work, marketing and sales effort, all may be required to locate or generate opportunities. This effort might need the support of brainstorming and scenario analyses. Other opportunities will arise more randomly. Companies might be invited to participate in joint ventures or someone may just have a bright idea. The source is relatively unimportant but it is important that opportunities are created. Companies need new opportunities but they must also be the right ones. The more options that a company creates the better chance it will have of finding one that will deliver real value.

Identifying opportunities should not be the preserve of business development, marketing or sales departments, and opportunities may not come in the form of recognisable big projects. Small changes in business practice or products will sometimes be of significant value to customers, out of all proportion to the apparent scale of change. Creative workshops with cross-functional teams should be held periodically. Ideas from value engineering exercises should be inspected for wider application.

Focus creativity for better value

However, creativity needs to be focused and all opportunities should be assessed using a well-designed process that is both robust and flexible. The process should provide a clear method as to how to judge opportunities and indicate when they should be judged and by whom. 'How' requires criteria to be set and the means and tools to assess the options against those criteria to be provided. Early and effective screening by an organised authority is an important business task; otherwise the following problems may develop:

- Options that are obviously unviable or of poor value are actively pursued or at least extensively assessed. In the worst scenario, they threaten the company's future when allowed to proceed.

- An opportunity is pursued that is viable but does not fit with the strategy and strengths needed to deliver the full benefits.

- Appropriate resources for implementation are not available or are wrongly diverted from other investments.

- The details presented in full appraisals divert attention and confuse the decision process. The main criteria for assessing options are overlooked by assumptions that criteria have already been met.

- Full appraisals consume costly resources. Direct costs and opportunity costs are incurred if resources are diverted from possibly better opportunities.

- Too many opportunities reduce the quality of reviews.

- Efforts are diverted from: considering a better option; increasing the value of another option; finding other opportunities (better than any of the options under review).

- Rejecting options becomes more difficult with time. Teams assigned to detailed appraisals develop commitments to their venture and do not present balanced findings. Vested interests lead to 'turf wars'.

DEFINE THE OPTIONS

Develop outline proposals

In order to assess options, it is necessary to provide reasonable preliminary measures of costs and benefits to be used in the screening process. Similarly, risks need to be identified so that the balance of risks and rewards can be assessed. An understanding of the techniques explained in this chapter will help establish what level of detail is appropriate.

All major appraisal needs should be established first and outline technical, operational, marketing and financing proposals must adequately demonstrate how, in principle, the proposal will work in the face of uncertainties. It is recommended that a thorough qualitative analysis of the issues is done before developing detailed measures. Often appraisals start with a financial model that then determines how the appraisal proceeds. The model may raise important issues but these may not be the most important.

The proposal should identify the major benefits to be delivered and the costs to be expected, and should establish some outline measures to define scale-order values of those benefits and costs and the effects of major risks in relation to the business at large, even if the values are only subjective. Attention should focus on what the variables are and the degree of variability rather than seeking to calculate an exact value.

> **Attention should focus on what the variables are and the degree of variability rather than seeking to calculate an exact value.**

Capture the major costs, benefits and risks

Outline proposals and metrics need to be recorded along with the major elements of the costs, benefits and risks including major assumptions and uncertainties about the proposals. Assumptions and uncertainties highlight intrinsic weaknesses in an outline proposal, such as unclear solutions or measures. Identification of primary strategies to mitigate risks should be accompanied by preliminary decisions on the best approach. It is important to record this information in a register of costs, benefits and risks, as shown in Figure 4.1, for later use. The register needs to distinguish between assumptions, uncertainties and risks and rank the factors in terms of relative value within each option.

Fig. 4.1 Cost/benefit/risk register

Costs/Benefits/Risks Register

Option	Benefits		Costs		Risks		Comments
A Build new plant in Asia	Local access to markets	5	High capex	6	Market bias	3	Assumption: local product improves marketing
	Low unit opex	4			Political obstacles	5	Country dependent
					Market overcapacity	5	Asia capacity unknown
B Expand UK plant	Export to Asia market	2	High unit opex	4	Import restrictions	6	Country dependent
	Low capex	3	UK taxes	3	Planning consent	1	Assumption: existing consent available
	Project/quality control	2	Limited Asia market capture	2			
			Capex	2			
			Disruption	1			

Scoring: 1=Low to 6=High

DESIGN THE SCREENING PROCESS

Define judgement conditions and criteria

At this stage of appraisal, the primary evaluation objective is to test whether an identified opportunity passes some high-level conditions to warrant a full appraisal. The conditions demonstrate that an opportunity meets both the positive objectives set by the strategy and complies with any established constraints including avoiding unacceptable strategic risks. An opportunity may be assessed for its own particular value, but it must also be assessed against the total portfolio.

The usual conditions with which an opportunity must comply, but not in any order of significance, are that:

- it is likely to provide a good return;
- it provides an acceptable balance between investment risk and reward;
- it fits within the company strategy and company strengths;
- it meets portfolio objectives and priorities;
- it satisfies portfolio risk and reward criteria;
- it does not present unacceptable risks;
- it is the best among the opportunities available;
- it is reasonably likely to proceed where external forces may govern.

At this stage of appraisal, the primary evaluation objective is to test whether an identified opportunity passes some high-level conditions to warrant a full appraisal.

Organise the judgement process

To determine whether these fundamental conditions are met, more detailed criteria must be established to define them better. Techniques must also be developed to evaluate options against those criteria. Three key stages are followed:

- eliminate options – develop critical pass criteria;
- compare options – develop preference and portfolio criteria;
- assess probability of proceeding of preferred options.

ELIMINATE OPTIONS

Develop critical pass criteria

By first establishing and applying critical pass criteria, it is very possible that a prospect can be rightly rejected for several reasons without need for comparison. The nature of such reasons include:

- failure to fit strategic aims;
- unacceptable technologies involved;
- exclusion of selected markets or clients;
- limits on commercial terms;
- exceeding chosen maximum size for investments (either in total or in relation to market or product areas);
- failure to meet minimum size of investment.

Such criteria may first be established independently, but they may also evolve from development of the structured preference modelling technique used to compare options, as discussed in the following sections.

However, additional critical pass criteria may also be applied which are not necessarily identified within the comparison process, in particular management policy to limit exposure to certain types of risks and to balance the portfolio. Examples are:

- percentage total exposure to new technology or products;
- percentage total exposure to a customer or market;
- percentage total exposure to a geographic/political region.

By first establishing and applying critical pass criteria, it is very possible that a prospect can be rightly rejected for several reasons without need for comparison.

COMPARE OPTIONS

Develop value preference and portfolio criteria

An effective method to compare different options when complex criteria and differing scenarios must be balanced is to build a value 'preference' model. The steps are as follows:

1 Identify and construct a tree of judgement criteria.

2 Weight criteria for their relative effect on the total business.

3 Score options against each of the criteria according to the values ascribed to their individual costs, benefits and risks.

4 Assess the total worth of different options by arithmetical combination.

5 Establish preferred options according to their relative worth.

6 Conduct sensitivity analyses against the weightings and scores.

In step 1, a hierarchical tree of the principal criteria that affect the business is first developed. An example of a preference tree for strategic criteria is shown in Figure 4.2. The branches shown represent all the major cost, benefit and risk factors affecting the business at large, which may be established from earlier strategic analyses.

Fig. 4.2 Tree of principal risk and reward criteria

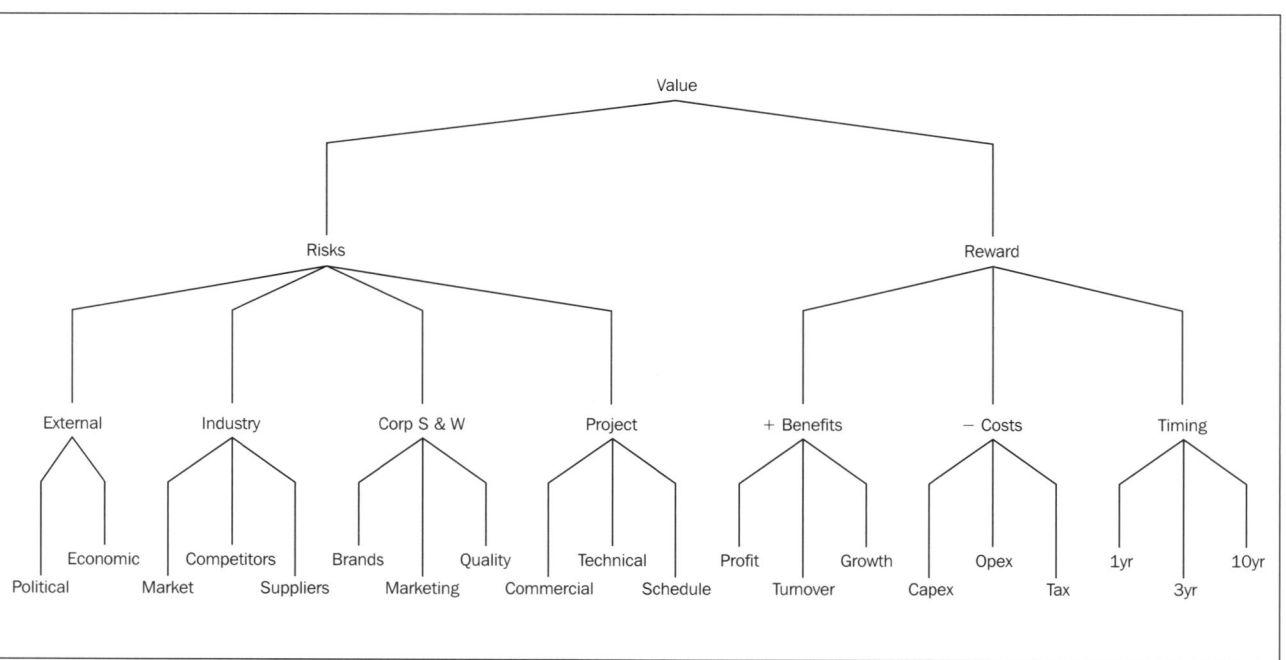

In step 2, criteria are weighted relative to each other as shown in the case of benefits in column two of Figure 4.3. For example, opportunities may offer different benefits to a business which accrue over different timescales. Therefore, short-term profitability is likely to be weighted higher than growth and benefits received within one year valued higher than long-term benefits. In step 3, the different options are scored against each of the criteria, as shown in columns three to six of Figure 4.3. Some options may not score against all criteria and baselines and minimum and maximum conditions for some criteria may need to be set, which may be developed from the critical pass criteria established earlier.

Fig. 4.3 Weighting criteria and scoring options

Criteria: Benefits		Options:				
	Weight	Own plant in Asia	JV in Asia	Licence technology	Expand in UK	Cum wt
Profit margin	70	80	60	90	40	11.7
Turnover	50	90	100	22	51	8.3
Growth	30	80	100	20	30	5.0
	Total	83	81	53	42	25.0

> An immediate benefit provided by this technique is that different options can be readily compared, even though options may be judged by different criteria and some criteria are subjective and/or not easily quantifiable.

Assessing value and risk versus reward

An immediate benefit provided by this technique is that different options can be readily compared, even though options may be judged by different criteria and some criteria are subjective and/or not easily quantifiable. A total score of net value can be obtained for each option by combining all the factors and scores together using simple arithmetic. The scores need have no absolute value, but they provide a useful ranking of different options as illustrated in Figure 4.4. This example shows the total relative values derived for each option when scores against all the weighted criteria in the preference tree are summed, not just those scores shown for benefit criteria in Figure 4.3.

Another important feature is that the tree in this investment screening model is structured to incorporate all issues under the main headings of risk and reward, which are the key factors that must be balanced to demonstrate whether an investment is attractive within a portfolio. Construction of a value model enables a business to establish a qualitative view of its portfolio with its own 'frontier' of most 'attractive' investments against which all investments may be assessed. This is illustrated in Figure 4.5.

> Construction of a value model enables a business to establish a qualitative view of its portfolio with its own 'frontier' of most 'attractive' investments.

Fig. 4.4 Comparing net preference values of options

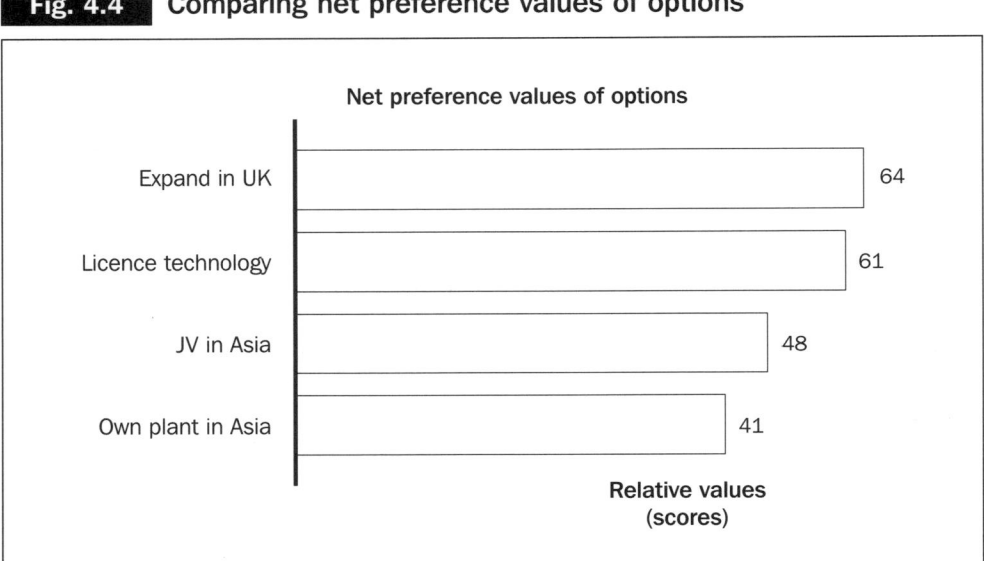

Fig. 4.5 Assessing risks and rewards of options in a portfolio

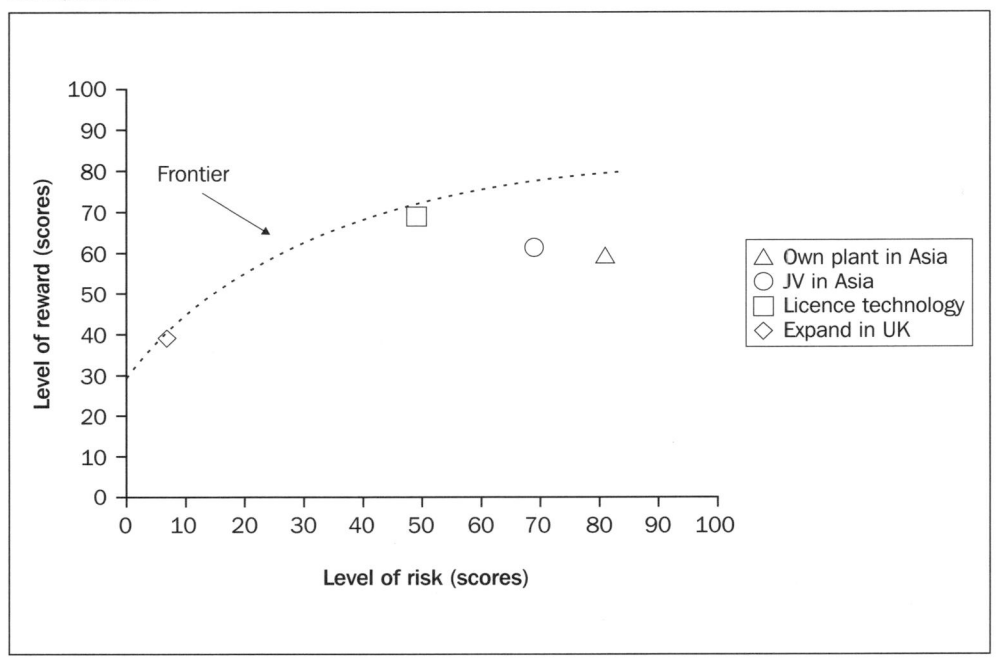

Apart from those investments that fit on the 'frontier', other decisions can be made about existing or potential investments that may lie in other areas in the risk/reward envelope. The reader is referred to Figure 3.7 (see p. 71) for an earlier discussion of this topic.

Investments may be categorised by their level of risk. It is very helpful for a business to establish an integrated view of how many and which projects in the business are considered to be high-risk and why. Similarly, the business may assess which projects are considered to be providing poor value. Relative comparison of new opportunities against the portfolio may even determine that none of the options considered are worth pursuing and that the business should seek better opportunities.

Seek to improve prospects

Valuing options is not the only objective of value/preference modelling. Investigating the different weightings and scorings applied can help establish measures to optimise existing good options or identify the scale of action required to improve poor options to acceptable levels. This analysis may help focus attention on where or whether feasibility studies or other direct actions should be planned as the first part of a full investment appraisal. An early understanding of the optimisation criteria may also permit selected poor options that might otherwise be rejected and forgotten to be retained for future review if conditions could possibly change.

ASSESS THE PROBABILITY OF PROCEEDING

The final stage of screening a prospect should address the probability that the prospect will not proceed, even if it is of interest and value to the business. Major risks to the advancement of the project should be considered. For example, if investment depends on a change in government legislation, the probability of that change occurring should be estimated. When comparing options their relative values should be considered with such probabilities factored in. This form of analysis is addressed again more fully at the end of Chapter 5, to determine whether costs should be committed prior to proceeding to develop a prospect. However, it is equally appropriate to consider at this stage whether the costs of an appraisal should be sanctioned if a prospect only has a low chance of advancing.

MANAGE AND COMMUNICATE

Communicate and apply strategic analyses

Fortunately, development of this form of screening process can easily use previous strategic analyses without much need to regenerate ideas. Information about the criteria is obtainable from the strategic register of risks, uncertainties and assumptions and SWOT analyses developed in Chapter 3, and weighting will be determined by the strategic objectives established including portfolio issues. Note that main preference tree headings for risks and rewards represent the 'opportunities' and 'threats' identified in a strategic SWOT analysis, and headings are also included for 'strengths' and 'weaknesses' which represent the means to manage opportunities and threats. These have been balanced together on the risks side, which is possible because the analysis is only relative. Using previous strategic assessments, the technique aids communication of strategic issues by capturing, prioritising and presenting them in a user-friendly way. At the same time, information about the options themselves is obtainable from the summary cost/benefit/risk register, developed earlier in this chapter.

Involve senior management

The screening technique is enhanced today by the availability of dynamic analytical and graphical software tools to permit easy facilitation of group sessions and analysis at board level. Such tools can accommodate both hard and soft criteria that can be quantified in either specific or relative units of measure. Answers can be evaluated and displayed quickly and with clarity, including sensitivities to changes in weightings and scores.

Direct accessibility by the board to this form of dynamic analysis also permits radical options to be considered within a controlled audience. A high level of security is an important consideration when conducting strategic reviews and senior management are understandably concerned not to allow information to be leaked externally. This is particularly important if they are considering some options that might frighten investors if taken out of context.

Establish responsibilities in screening

Those responsible for defining the business strategy should define and weight the criteria for an investment option model. The apparent simplicity of this technique, however, can easily lead to misuse. Many major factors are embraced so that a carefully controlled approach is required to obtain reliable results and experience should be gained with an expert facilitator. For example, a distinction can be made between risks that cannot be influenced yet have largely been accepted within the strategy, and those that require controlling or influencing. Many of the former risks may be external risks that are accepted in order to participate in business generally or in a specific industry. Under the right conditions, some risks may sometimes be ignored in the analysis if all options are equally affected.

Manage the screening process

Establishing a clear management procedure controls how these processes are applied. Some recommendations are set out below.

- Develop procedures that are flexible to account for the random timing of submissions and the different scale and nature of different opportunities.

- Assign an approving body with sufficient authority to consider screening assessments. This may be a group composed of board members.

- Establish conditions that determine when the group needs to meet and when submissions must be made to them.

- Issue details to all members for quick comment, guidance, authorisation or rejection in cases where the whole group do not need to meet.

- Consider a practice of convening for all proposals above a certain size or if any member initially rejects a proposal.

- Establish a standardised form of presentation to communicate findings from screening assessments that are intentionally high level.

CHAPTER REVIEW

- Strategic opportunities may be identified directly from strategic analysis work, but at other times businesses will need to create opportunities to pursue their general strategies. They should plan to generate opportunities in controlled creative workshops and other forums by applying techniques similar to those that aid risk identification and assessment, including the use of brainstorming and ranking. These foster an outward looking attitude that challenges assumptions within the business.

- Opportunities may also arise randomly and require processes and procedures to control assessments and limit resource use on full investment appraisals. These include screening all opportunities initially against the major objectives, constraints and risks determined by the strategy.

- It is necessary to capture and communicate strategic factors in a useful manner, in order to define critical pass criteria to eliminate obvious non-contenders as early as possible. Thereafter, when there are several prospects, they should be assessed for their relative worth against each other, and in all cases against the business norms. Value preference modelling provides a suitable method to do this, and, if properly structured, provides a virtual portfolio view of the business in which different ventures can be benchmarked for their relative risk and reward.

■ As part of a standardised process, cost/benefit/risk registers used in conjunction with the above method initially define the major advantages and disadvantages offered by the prospects. This information and analysis then provides a focused starting point for the commencement of full investment appraisals for appropriate prospects.

5

Stage 3: Full investment appraisals

INTRODUCTION

The previous screening stage prioritises prospects, but only subjective values of major costs, benefits and risks are used. Any prospect, even if perceived as a good opportunity, now needs to be assessed thoroughly. Because of the previous screening, detailed analyses and decision-making can now focus on selected candidates for investment. This should allow higher quality analyses to be conducted and/or reduce the total cost of full appraisals. Focusing more structured effort on risk assessment, tactical appraisal and planning provides the opportunity to improve prospects at the beginning, when major factors can be more easily changed.

This chapter presents methods to capture, map and model risks in financial cash flow assessments that combine uncertainty registers and Monte Carlo simulation. It also covers methods to estimate venture adjusted discount factors, assessment of findings using confidence levels and setting conditions for sanction. The following topics are presented:

■ *Planning the appraisal* Objectives, scope and methodologies for conducting an appraisal.

■ *Defining the proposal and risks* Tasks to define a proposal and conduct a qualitative risk assessment.

■ *Developing a risked cash flow model* Special considerations when building a risked cash flow model.

■ *Estimating discount factors* Reasons and methods for adjusting discount factors.

■ *Assessing findings and improving prospects for investments* Assessments of findings from an integrated risked cash flow model against business objectives; measures to enhance prospects and mitigate risks.

■ *Sanctioning investments* Conditions for sanction including targets and contingency levels.

PLAN THE APPRAISAL

Define the scope and methodologies

At the end of the structured screening process, a brief for a full appraisal should have been developed. The brief should indicate what needs to be appraised, in what order of priority, by when, by whom, at what cost and how the process itself will be reviewed as it progresses. Regardless of its size, an appraisal should be treated as a project in its own right and be properly project-managed.

At this stage, it is common for a business to evaluate a prospect principally by estimating a single base value from discounted cash flows for the project. Sensitivities to some factors may also be inspected and other wider matters considered. If the initial NPV estimated is positive, or if the IRR exceeds a hurdle rate, the prospect may have a good chance of being authorised. However, exclusive reliance on standard discount factors and selected scenarios leaves management without a sufficiently rigorous means of accounting for risk.

An outline programme of the work required to conduct a reliable appraisal of risks entails specific tasks:

Exclusive reliance on standard discount factors and selected scenarios leaves management without a sufficiently rigorous means of accounting for risk.

- Develop the technical, operational, marketing and financing proposals further including a preliminary cash flow model.

- Conduct a full qualitative risk and opportunity assessment, including risk identification, scoring and risk response plans and distinguish risks to be managed within the appraisal period.

- Conduct and control studies required to address major uncertainties.

- Identify quantitative measures to be assessed.

- Conduct a full quantitative risk and opportunity assessment. Map risks to the cash flow model and model with variable and conditional logic and variable estimates.

- Review quantitative risk analysis results and compare options.

- Review results against an overview of the strategic criteria.

- Authorise or reject options.

- Set objectives for pursuit.

Even if only one prospect has passed the screening process, it is advisable to assess more than that option alone. At least two preferred options should be assessed, together with a reference case. The latter may be the baseline case of 'doing nothing' or some other suitable option as a basis for comparison.

DEFINE THE PROPOSAL AND RISKS

Develop a preliminary cash flow model

Definition of the base proposal and preparation of base estimates require further development of all plans, including technical implementation, asset requisition, operational, marketing and financing plans. Development of a preliminary model of the cash flows before commencing the full risk assessment aids this task and captures many of the issues in one location, The common major elements in an investment cash flow model are:

- revenues (including source factors such as market demand and pricing);
- costs (including capital costs and operating/working capital costs);
- residual/terminal values and/or divestment costs;
- timing of revenues and costs;
- tax costs;
- inflation and discount factors.

A preliminary model will deliver an initial monetary value for the prospect but this should neither be widely distributed nor presented as the anticipated value as expectations may wrongly become fixed. Presenting it simply as one possible central value provides a relative scale of the values involved and a basis for measuring relative impacts from risks. In this context, factoring for inflation and discounting can be temporarily ignored and present money values used.

Capture risks

Once a proposal has been adequately defined, the first stage of the risk analysis can start with identification of the risks. Some will already have been identified if a cost/benefit/risk register was prepared for the screening stage but it is essential to carry out further exploration.

The appraisal team should conduct a fresh brainstorming session to identify detailed risks to the investment prospect. Without some form of creative exploration of the issues, risks from underlying assumptions may be overlooked. The team's exploration of possible risks needs to inspect *all* areas addressed in the plans and in the preliminary cash flow model, and will benefit from the use of prompt lists from various categories. The team should capture the risks in an investment uncertainty register (risk register) with full details for each risk as follows:

- id/title/description/source/type/phase;
- impacts: revenue/cost/time/performance;
- probability/score;
- risk to whom/influence/risk reduction proposal/cost/responsibility;
- risk modelling treatment (i.e. how/if).

A sample record from a risk register is shown in Figure 5.1.

> The team's exploration of possible risks needs to inspect *all* areas addressed in the plans.

Fig. 5.1 Example risk register record

RISK REGISTER			
Client:	UK Industries		
Project:	Asia	**Date**	2001

Risk ID/Title	A17c Competitors build new plants leading to overcapacity
Description	Perceived growth in market may lead to similar new plant builds by competitors leading to overcapacity and reduction in market price

Source	External	**Phase**	Operation
Area	Industry	**Risk To Whom**	Corporate

Impacts		*Impact Scores*
Revenue	Planned utilisation reduced and market share and pricing affected	High
Costs	–	–
Time	–	–
Performance	–	–
	Likelihood	High
	Overall Score	6

Influence	Low		
Risk Reduction	Conduct marketing demand and competitor analysis to reduce uncertainty		
	Investigate historic trends. Model/simulate variability		
	Develop signalling strategy to deter rogue investment		
	Consider JV options to reduce competition		
	Delay/accelerate build?		
Cost	£ within appraisal budget	**Effect**	–
Manager	Regional Business Manager		

Modelling	Link separate analysis Risk Model as variable inputs

To create a register, a summary title and a unique identification number for each risk must be provided. It is also important to describe each risk and its impact in more detail to ensure full understanding and traceability. Categorising risks by source and when they have effect provides a focus on the type of risks faced and priorities can be set by ranking the risks, using the methodology already described in Chapter 2. A weighted algorithm is used to combine simple gradings of Low, Medium or High for measures of impact and probability of occurrence for each risk. Initially, impacts may be usefully and more easily considered separately in terms of impact on time, cost, revenue and performance, although all impacts may ultimately translate into impacts on net value. Responses to risks and responsibilities for their management are added to provide a focus on the actions required to improve a prospect. Finally, all risks are mapped to a quantitative risk model that will verify the likely impacts of all risks combined and details of how the risks have been modelled are recorded in the register for accountability.

Manage appraisal stage risks

Some risks will require management attention in the appraisal stage. Investigations of major uncertainties may be necessary to reduce them and the results alone may determine whether the prospect is viable or not. For example, regulatory approval may be a precondition for investment. It is important to distinguish between such risks and ensure that management attention is focused on needs, by producing summaries from the register of the major issues. A summary table of the risks ranked by score and listing risk mitigation proposals provides a good starting point as shown in Figure 5.2.

Responsibilities for managing each risk should be identified, although responsibility at this stage may be confined to establishing risk reduction or mitigation proposals until such time as the prospect is sanctioned. All proposals should be preliminarily costed, although later analyses will have to establish whether the benefits of applying the measures will outweigh their costs.

Address major uncertainties

It may be necessary to resolve or at least assess major uncertainties before fully defining a base proposal and constructing a final cash flow model. This may require separate qualitative studies and quantitative modelling of specific issues to provide input data for the cash flows. For instance, studies of future consumer demand and/or market share may be required. These major uncertainties may determine the course of the appraisal, owing to the relative influence the data may have on results compared with other uncertainties. Detailed development or analysis of the whole proposal may be inappropriate until additional studies have been completed.

An appropriate balance should be established early on between the effort required to estimate all the different elements in the cash flow and their respective levels of variability and sensitivity. Increased accuracy in one area may deliver

> It may be necessary to resolve or at least assess major uncertainties before fully defining a base proposal and constructing a final cash flow model.

> An appropriate balance should be established early on between the effort required to estimate all the different elements in the cash flow and their respective levels of variability and sensitivity.

little extra benefit if inputs for another major influencing factor remain highly uncertain and variable. If additional special estimating or modelling is required, it should be developed with a view as to how the issues and uncertainties will be represented in a final risked cash flow model.

Fig. 5.2 Example risk register summary table

Summary Risk Table – Asia Project

ID	Risk title	Score	Influence	Risk reduction/Prospect enhancement plans
A17b	Demand below expected growth reduces price	6	Low	Monitor demand growth in line with capacity build. Grow product envelope.
A17c	Competitors build new plants leading to overcapacity	6	Low	Conduct marketing demand and competitor analysis to reduce uncertainty. Investigate historic trends. Model/simulate variability. Develop signalling strategy to discourage rogue investment. Consider JV options to reduce competition. Delay/accelerate build?
A24a	Accuracy of price estimate mechanism	6	Medium	Track performance historically. Model & simulate variability. Consider market/price segmentation effect on total revenue.
A05	Technology development unproven	6	Medium	Resolve technology issues before sanction. Consider effect on IRR of delaying sanction. Assign task team for special development through project life.
A07	Taxation regime including tax holiday removed	5	Low	Negotiate with government in advance. Identify win/win concessions. Signal alternative investment opportunities.
A13	Imports from Europe affected	5	Medium	Model global market vs global capacity. Delay Asia or USA investment?
A24b	Accuracy of capital cost estimates incl land	4	High	Country factors to be defined by regional office. Model IRR using variances on estimates.
A33a	JV risks – delay of agreement (or no agreement)	4	Low	Identify JV risks separately. Commence early negotiations. Careful deal structuring. Monitor JV relationship as separate performance target. (Introduce 3rd party to neutralise disruption? – but beware further risk.)
A22c	Inadequate logistics	4	Low	Forward planning and appointment of local manager.
A24c	Accuracy of operating cost estimates	3	High	Country costs to be defined by regional office. Model IRR using variances.
A28	Materials supply contract not economic	3	Medium	Resolve before sanction. Source alternative supplies.
A03	Availability of resources in competition with other projects	2	Low	Identify resource requirements and source early.
A06	Currency fluctuations, relative inflation	2	None	Develop specific treasury risk management measures. Structure funding to minimise exposure.
A08	Import duties raised on capital equipment	2	None	Lobby for exemption from future duties.
A11	Licensing/permit delays	2	None	Identify/plan all applications/timings. Manage at regional director level. Draft contracts for possible acceleration.
A24e	Accuracy of programme estimates	2	High	Detail JV/early tasks and resolve monsoon issues. Obtain country data. Model IRR using variances on duration estimates.
A27	Inadequacy of construction suppliers	1	Medium	Implement good prequalification plans to vet suppliers. Ensure risks are carried by appropriate parties. Identify key risks and source externally if necessary.

DEVELOP A FULLY RISKED CASH FLOW MODEL

Nature of a risked cash flow model

A risked cash flow model uses Monte Carlo simulation techniques and dynamic modelling to represent all major risks and estimating variability, including that of time, within a quantitative model of future investment cash flows. The objective is to establish a distribution of the possible values for the return that will provide a better appraisal of the central estimate and of the variability represented by the uncertainties. Decision-makers should not rely on estimates prepared without Monte Carlo analysis to provide a good appraisal of a probable central value or on selected scenarios to show the practical range or value of alternative outcomes.

The full techniques for risk model building discussed in Chapter 2 should be applied. Important points to remember are set out below.

1 Prepare a high-level schedule for the venture and model the major uncertainties associated with possible changes in the timing of cash flows.

2 Map risks and opportunities from the investment uncertainty register.

3 Include mitigation measures that would be applied if risks materialised.

4 Identify and apply major correlations between variables.

5 Hold a team review to inspect risk mapping and risk modelling of inputs. Give special consideration to potential risks in each of the major elements:

- economic/marketing estimates for demand/revenue;

- major cost estimates;

- residual/terminal values and taxes;

- time dependencies;

- inflation and discount factors.

The importance of varying time

Owing to the significant influence that discounting has on cash flows, the uncertain timing of different cash flows may be as important in determining the final value of an investment as the variability of the different elements themselves. Therefore develop a summary-linked schedule estimating the timing of critical activities in the planned investment programme, with variable and conditional inputs relating to the timing of cash flows.

Decision-makers should not rely on estimates prepared without Monte Carlo analysis to provide a good appraisal of a probable central value or on selected scenarios to show the practical range or value of alternative outcomes.

The uncertain timing of different cash flows may be as important in determining the final value of an investment as the variability of the different elements themselves.

The importance of correlating variables

Another critical task in a risked cash flow model is to correlate the major variables. If appropriate correlation is ignored the results may seriously understate the range of reasonably foreseeable outcomes.

Previous strategic analysis, assessing diversification in the business, should be referred to if available. It is best that consistent organisation views are applied rather than *ad hoc* interpretations made by different analysts, although corporate views should be challenged if necessary. Similarly, consistent corporate advice is required for some key factors in the model, such as inflation factors. Correlation with factors specific to each investment will, however, need to be judged separately.

If appropriate correlation is ignored the results may seriously understate the range of reasonably foreseeable outcomes.

DISCOUNT FACTORS

Before considering how best to use and interpret findings from a risked cash flow model, it is important to understand more conventional methods of discounting for time and risks along with methods to improve estimation of discount factors and understand their limitations.

Discounting cash flows, NPV and IRR

In a simple model of investment finances, we could directly subtract the predicted total costs from the total revenues to establish a total net value. If the value is greater than zero we could say that the investment will increase the company's worth. However, if investors lend money they lose the opportunity to use that money to purchase goods or services that could deliver benefits immediately and so they lose utility over the intervening period. This is referred to as an 'opportunity cost', which leads to money markets offering a financial premium to lenders in return for the loss of utility. Investors are subsequently rewarded by the potential increased utility that they may purchase in the future from the greater sum they will receive. In turn, this leads to a direct relationship between time and the value of money, whereby investors assign a greater value to money they hold today than to money promised tomorrow, even if the promise of receiving it in the future is free of risk. Conversely, therefore, a sum received tomorrow is valued less than if the same sum is held today.

A simple summing of costs and revenues is, therefore, not appropriate because the timing of cash flows changes their relative values. Instead, the commonest method to derive a comparable worth for an investment is to convert all cash flows to their equivalent values in the present. This may be done by applying a discount factor to each of the values, compounded for the number of periods from the present when they are received. The discount factor is the opposite of the factor that would have to be applied to the present values for them to grow to their future values. This is known as the Discounted Cash Flow (DCF) method and when the discounted costs and revenues are summed, an NPV (net present value) is derived. Provided that the value of NPV is larger than zero, the project will increase in net worth. Alternatively, we can find the rate where NPV is just equal to zero, or the IRR (internal rate of return).

Discounting for risk

Most investments face risks and to attract investors' money higher monetary rewards must be offered when risks are higher. All risk-averse investors value money held today more than money (of the same present value) offered uncertainly tomorrow. As above, there is a further opportunity cost attached. Therefore, any future expected return is valued less if risk is attached to it. In general, the markets also take the view that the longer the risk is held then the less the value of that return, and future cash flows are usually further discounted to account for risk.

Consequently, discount factors that are usually applied to investment cash flows embrace several factors. The three principle components are:

- a 'risk-free' rate for basic utility;
- a rate for inflation, because money is devalued with time when there is inflation;
- a risk premium reflecting the risk of the investment.

Generally, the risk-free discount rate and the inflation discount rate should be common to all businesses in the same economic environment, although a little more will be said later about discounting for inflation. On the other hand, the risk premium factor will depend on the nature of the business and different premiums should apply for different businesses since they carry different overall risks. Because discounting in this manner is accepted practice, pragmatic methods to estimate different factors will be considered next. Estimation is difficult, however, as we will see, and there are faults within the method. An alternative method, using the risked cash flow model to account for risk *without* discounting using a normal premium for risk, will be examined later.

Corporate discount factors

Complex financial theories have been developed to establish what discount rate should be used by investors and businesses but they prove difficult to apply and are unpopular in practice among businesses. In some cases, businesses rely on other measures such as the payback period to assess risk, but these are really only credible if they also take account of the discounting principle and should only be used as an adjunct to the main risk assessment.

Where the discounting method is used, the most preferred approach is to apply the company's Weighted Average Cost of Capital (WACC) as the discount factor. This is the combined cost of capital financed from both debt and equity and may be calculated by the company itself. The value of WACC varies for different industries and for different firms. The difference between WACC and the risk-free rate reflects the requirement noted above for an element to account for inflation and to reward investment risk. However, standard discount factors such as WACC are based on historical valuations of returns and do not allow for future investment patterns or individual investments with differing risks. There are some obvious shortcomings:

- the future value of WACC may change owing to market conditions;
- changes in inflation change the cost of debt and equity and the value of WACC;
- the value of WACC changes if the debt/equity balance changes;
- the market may expect different risk premiums with different investments.

An alternative modern option is to use the Capital Asset Pricing Model (CAPM) and establish an individual 'beta' value for the business or investment. The beta is a risk measurement factor based on the covariance of returns from investments with those of other general investments in the market, and operates in a broadly similar manner as a conventional discount factor. Estimation can be complex and requires a greater understanding of the general market than most businesses possess. For many companies, it is advisable that a bureau that specialises in calculating betas for different businesses is used if this approach is preferred.

> **Standard discount factors such as WACC are based on historical valuations of returns and do not allow for future investment patterns or individual investments with differing risks.**

Systemic and specific risks

Financial theories assert that adjustments of betas or other discount factors should be based on the effects of systemic risks only and should not include specific risks. The market will supposedly not reward investors for unnecessarily bearing risks that can be diversified away.

These theories are commonly accepted intellectually, but businesses are often reluctant to apply them in practice because they are difficult to calculate, are based on imperfect assumptions, are not sufficiently proven and, occasionally, seem counter-intuitive or contradictory. Similar advice for smaller firms recognises that their shareholders may not be able to diversify fully, but recommends that discount factors should be adjusted to include specific risk as well. Moreover, companies find that estimating discount factors is difficult enough without attempting to distinguish between systemic and specific risks. Within a business context, therefore, where adjustment of discount factors is recognised to be appropriate (and generally it is), adjustments are quite reasonably based on the total risks affecting any investment.

Venture-based discount factors

Clearly, estimation of a reasonable discount factor for individual ventures is as fraught as estimating a p50 value to discount, but some attempt should be made rather than relying on WACC or some other average value. Without resorting to overly theoretical expositions, the alternative is to recognise some of the principles that the CAPM and other financial theories advance but estimate in-house an investment-specific discount factor based on WACC, adjusted to account for different risks. This is a pragmatic approach but it should be recognised that some baselines and logical rules must first be established to minimise subjectivity. The first stage is to develop a structured view of the factors contributing to a venture-based risk premium. Previous work to identify major risks and screening criteria, as discussed in the previous chapter, will help establish a template of main headings and subheadings for major risks and business norms. Figure 5.3 provides an example of two subheadings and shows how an investment can be assessed against these subheadings using a simple grading.

Fig. 5.3 Discount factor adjustment estimating table

Criteria		Grading					Scoring		
Item	Detail	−2	−1	0	2	4	Score	Weight	Risk
Suppliers	Industry-wide								
	Bargaining strength	Very weak	Weak	Average	Strong	Very strong	2	0.03	0.06
	Capabilities	Very simple	Simple	Normal	Stretched	Challenging	−1	0.03	−0.03
	Capacities	Excess capacity	Spare	Normal	Stretched	Excess demand	4	0.03	0.12
Technology or service composition	Critical or substantial proportion of solution								
	Complexity	Very simple	Simple	Average	More complex	Very complex	2	0.05	0.10
	Experience	Routine and well defined	Common experience	Core expertise	New but proven elsewhere	New and unproven	2	0.05	0.10

By weighting the risk headings and combining the scorings as produced for screening options, a relative total risk score for an investment prospect may be established, which may then be related to a scale of standard adjustment factors to be applied to the discount factor. An example of adjustment factors based on risk scorings is shown in Figure 5.4.

Fig. 5.4 Discount factor scale adjustment table

Risk score	Risk premium WACC +%
−2	−1.0
−1	−0.5
0	0.0
+1	+1.0
+2	+2.5
+3	+4.0
+4	+6.0

Developing the scoring template and the scale for adjustment factors should be done by those responsible for determining the strategy. However, scoring of the risks against the template and establishment of unique factors for each venture may be done by the venture team using the risks and scorings already recorded in the specific venture risk registers.

The greatest difficulty lies in establishing a baseline for the weightings of different headline risk factors and translating them into different discount adjustment factors. Unfortunately, both subjectivity and a trial and error approach are involved, but the following stages are recommended:

■ Cash flows of previous investments by the business can be inspected and trials made using revised discount factors. One indicator to use is that the sum of previous investment cash flows discounted at revised rates should remain close to the sum of all those cash flows discounted at the current value of WACC.

■ Selected investments whose nature differs from the core business can be compared with similar investments that are central to other businesses. WACCs for these other companies may be established and limits conceived for different risk profiles. This follows a principle similarly recommended when applying the CAPM method, which encounters the same difficulties.

■ Previous work developing a 'virtual' portfolio will help set boundaries by giving a comparative scale to different projects and the perception of their total risk.

■ Where integrated risk analyses have been conducted before, the variability in different investments may be inspected and benchmarks established for comparison with other benchmarks established above.

ASSESS INVESTMENT PROSPECTS

So far, methodologies have been proposed for building a risked cash flow model by identifying, mapping and simulating risks in order to provide a means of establishing a range of possible outcomes. This range provides better estimates of both a p50 value and of the variability. A methodology has also been proposed to provide a better estimate of an appropriate discount factor for risks (i.e. for variability). However, there are important issues to consider when combining discount factors and findings from risked cash flow models, as the possibility arises of double-counting risk.

Assessing NPV at the risk-free rate

By first discounting the cash flows, at the risk-free rate, to account for the value of money in time, a distribution of outcomes for NPV produced by the simulation model will now provide a reasonable p50 value for NPV as shown in Figure 5.5. According to theories of utility, if investors were risk-neutral, then this p50 value would suffice for average investors to decide whether the venture was acceptable or not. They would not need to apply a risk premium to the discount rate.

Fig. 5.5 Simple distribution of risk-free NPV outcomes

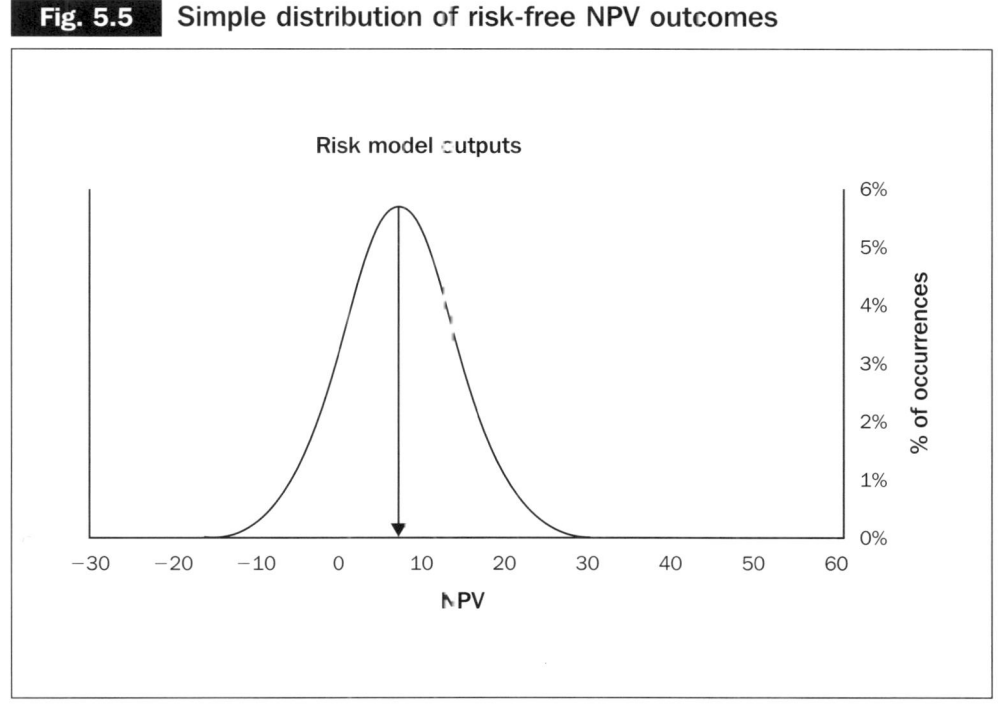

When investors do not have a distribution to tell them what the p50 value is, they must make further allowance for risk from estimating biases, whereas, by providing a better and more consistent means of estimating a p50 value, some risk is immediately removed.

Assessing NPV for inflation

If all future costs and revenues are estimated at present values and then inflated in money terms over time at the same rate, they should then be discounted at the same rate. The result would be that the net present value would simply equal the sum of the present values estimated before inflating so this stage could be ignored.

However, inflation may differ for different elements in the cash flow and the rates may be uncertain, e.g. different rates may apply for costs and revenue, for capital costs and working capital/operating costs, and over time. In a simulation model these concerns may be addressed by applying different rates for different elements as appropriate and using variable inputs for the possible rates over time. Then the total cash flows may be discounted back at an average rate that should be determined by the expectations of the market for investing in equities generally in relation to the prevailing economic environment. However, the market's expectations will also vary in relation to inflation risk so variable inputs can also be entered for the discount rate. If so, then the inflation rates applied and the discount rate used for inflation must be correlated. In this manner, inflation risks may be fully covered within the simulation. Using variable inputs for a partial (or total) discount factor and correlating with the cash flows can really only be applied for inflation and should not generally be attempted with other risks.

Assessing NPV for risk

We may now establish a distribution of outcomes discounted for the value of money over time and for inflation. Because of the risks represented in the distribution, a risk-averse investor would now seek to discount the cash flows more by applying an additional risk premium, perhaps calculated from a method previously considered. We may then obtain a single value of net worth for all factors and consider whether the venture is worth pursuing.

Only the p50 value in the new discounted distribution is likely to provide a valid estimation of market worth. Consider the minimum value in the initial distribution 'A' shown in Figure 5.6 (discounted using only the risk-free and inflation factors) which, provided all risks have been modelled, represents the worst case. If we could choose to offer this possibility to investors, they would be certain of achieving or bettering that outcome and they would not need to discount it for risk as it would have no downside. If, therefore, we discounted all the possible outcomes in our initial distribution additionally for risk, the minimum value in the new distribution 'A*' would turn out to be less than the minimum value in the first distribution, which would be anomalous.

Fig. 5.6 Simple distribution of risk-free and risked NPV outcomes

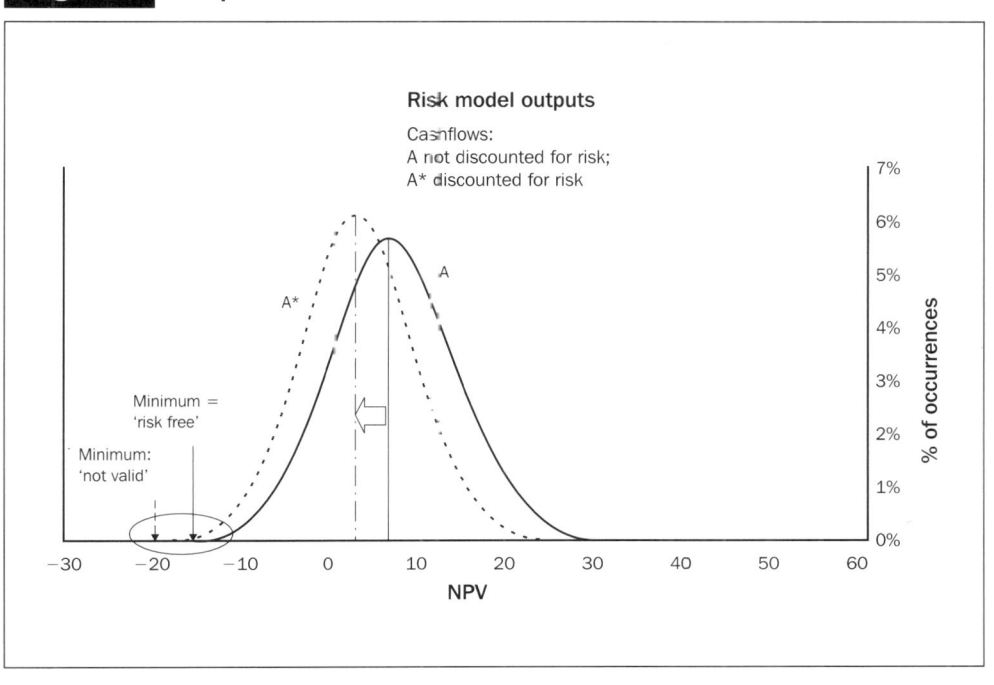

At first, this may seem to imply that a discounted distribution has limited use but the opposite may be shown to be true. Instead, we should reconsider the intention behind discounting for risk which requires us to look at output distributions in a different manner.

Assessing the confidence of NPV

The range of possible outcomes for the NPV of time discounted cash flows may also be presented in the form of a cumulative S-distribution curve which shows the confidence of achieving any particular value.

If we consider a project with a distribution of possible outcomes and we are risk-neutral, we may only require a 50 per cent confidence level of an acceptable outcome for the project, but if we are totally risk-averse, then we should require a 100 per cent confidence level of an acceptable outcome. If we are partially risk-averse, on the other hand, we might expect to require some intermediate confidence level for a project.

Consider the two projects, A and B, shown in Figure 5.7, with equal p50 values but different distributions of possible wealth outcomes, although both are symmetrical. Clearly, the spread of the distributions represents the level of risk and we can make decisions about these investments on this basis. In a risk-neutral case, either would be acceptable, but in a totally risk-averse case A would be preferred.

Fig. 5.7 Assessment of NPV outcomes by confidence level

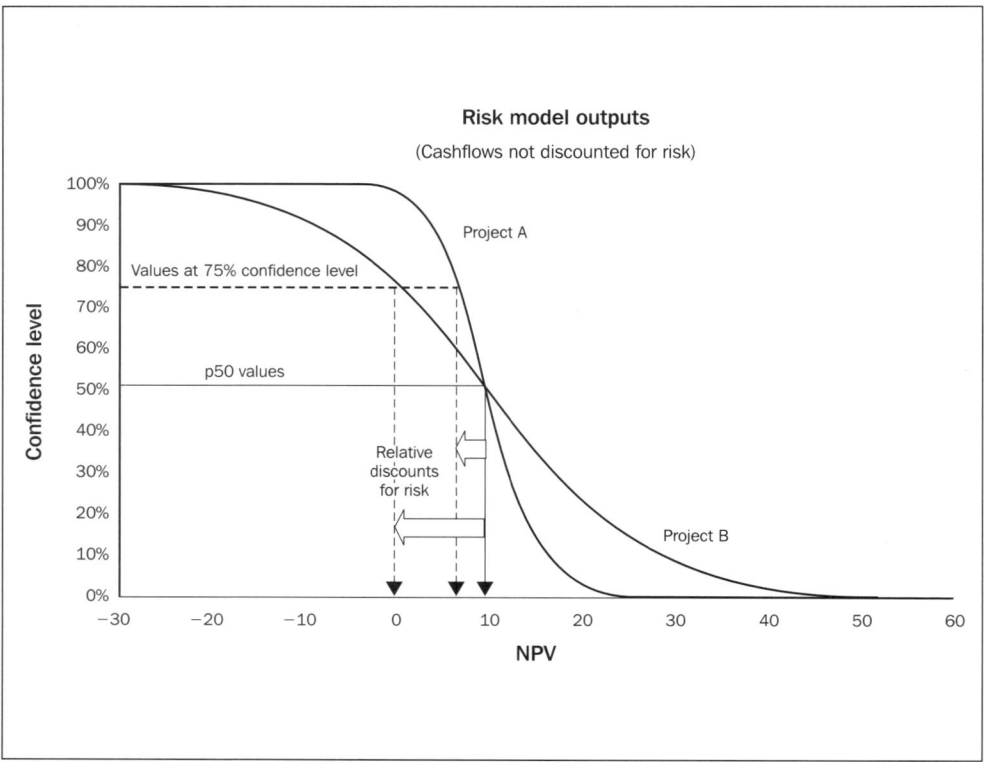

Rather than
establishing and
applying discount
factors for risk, we
may instead judge
opportunities against
the confidence level
we require to suit our
tolerance for risk.

Alternatively, at confidence levels above 50 per cent and up to 100 per cent, the intersecting values for A and B increasingly diverge from the p50 values, and from each other. Furthermore, the wider the spread of any distribution, then the wider the divergence from the p50 value at any given confidence level. These observations together show that at any given confidence level we can obtain modified values of NPV factored in proportion to the p50 value, the risk (i.e. the spread of the distribution) and our risk-aversion (i.e. our need for confidence). This relationship closely corresponds with the form of relationship between expected utility and expected wealth for a risk-averse investor.

We may therefore reasonably contend that, rather than establishing and applying discount factors for risk, we may instead judge opportunities against the confidence level we require to suit our tolerance for risk. Risks are appropriately accounted for in the distribution, so pertinent factoring for risk will be determined by the distributions themselves and the confidence level we set. These confidence levels may be applied consistently to compare one investment with another.

Establishing corporate confidence levels

This method potentially removes the need to establish a risk element in discount rates but introduces the alternative dilemma of what confidence level to set. This may largely be a matter for the company, but it should also bear some relationship to what confidence the general market requires. Unfortunately, this is not any better understood than knowing what discount rates are required by the market. The difference is that we know that it can only vary between two limits, which are 50 per cent and 100 per cent, if the market remains risk-averse. We also know that for most investments we do not require 100 per cent confidence. If businesses and investors always required this rate, then few projects would ever be sanctioned. Therefore, as for discount rates, some trial and error may be required but inspection of past and current investments can assist in this.

Limiting risk

However, there are special reasons as to why the confidence level should possibly change for individual investments and businesses which relate to the impact a proposed investment may have on the total portfolio. For new investments, any potential loss of wealth on the downside is valued more than the potential gain, but the rate of this differential usually increases as the size of the investment increases in proportion to the portfolio. Conversely, for investments that are relatively small to the portfolio, the differential is less. This change, relative to the portfolio, signifies an increasing aversion to risk as investments increase in proportion to the portfolio.

Consequently, an investment of a particular size and risk in absolute money terms will present a bigger risk to a small portfolio than to a large one, as one would expect. These guidelines should be applied equally to businesses' own portfolios and investments, particularly when they are neither large nor diversified, or when a new investment may dominate a portfolio.

Although an average market confidence level may be appropriate for outside investors with diversified portfolios who may have limited exposure to any one company, unless a company is itself large and diversified this market requirement may not be appropriate when making decisions within the company about whether to sanction a project or not. This advice is consistent with the recommendations given for adjusting discount rates in relation to the size of the company.

It is also very important to note that, as a higher confidence level in an outcome is required, the corresponding value from the distribution will be nearer to the tail end. Because the tail ends are more sensitive to the correctness of the input profiles, it is even more essential that all risks have been fully and properly included in the simulation.

Internal rate of return

Some companies prefer to use the IRR criteria to assess investments rather than NPV. Usually they wish to know that the p50 value of the IRR exceeds some hurdle rate. In traditional discounting practice, the hurdle rate is usually equivalent to the discount rate that would otherwise be used to discount the cash flows to derive a net present value. The same principles above may be applied and results should be presented in the form of a cumulative descending S-curve. Two conditions may then be considered at the same time.

- The first condition is that the probability of exceeding a hurdle rate based on a total discount factor, which may be an adjusted WACC value, may be inspected. The venture should be considered worthy if there is at least a 50 per cent chance that this hurdle rate is exceeded.

- At the same time, the probability of exceeding a hurdle rate based on the risk-free and inflation rates *only* may be considered. The venture may be considered worthy if the probability of exceeding this hurdle rate exceeds the corporate confidence level established as above.

If both conditions are reviewed, then both conditions should be met.

Payback

Another common criteria that businesses use to assess cash flows is the payback -period – the time when the curve of cumulative cash flows crosses the axis. Businesses often use this criteria because of a general reluctance to take on long-term risk, which may form one of their other critical acceptance criteria. They recognise several factors.

- Usually, the longer the period of exposure to risks the higher their potential exposure. Unforeseen events, that could undermine the venture, may be more likely to occur.

- External investors prefer earlier rewards and the costs of financing may increase.

Inspection of many cash flows for different investments show that curves can often be quite flat at the point where they cross the axis. If so, small changes in the inputs will significantly change the position of the curve and thus the payback period. The slope of the curve here is a good indicator of risk.

It is again easier to assess this risk more thoroughly by using the simulation risk analysis to predict a range of payback periods. Most simulation packages will produce a time plot of the cash flows to show a range of cash flow profiles at selected confidence levels. However, it is better practice to produce a specific distribution for the intersection date and assess it in the same manner as for NPV to allow for appropriate discount factors or confidence levels.

Timing of risks

Consideration of payback also focuses attention on the timing of payments, so it is important to note that the normal discounting method incorporates some failings in accounting for the timing of risks. This is best demonstrated by Figure 5.8.

Fig. 5.8　Time discounted risks

£m	Projects A or B (average cashflows)					
Year	1	2	3	4	5	Totals
Costs	10	5	5	5	10	35
Revenue		15	15	15		45
Totals	−10	10	10	10	−10	10 +/− 5

DF	NPV	Projects A & B					
10%	£7.31	Risk-free rate					
14%	£6.40	Incl. risk premium					
		Project A (minimum and maximum)					
10%	£2.76	−15	10	10	10	−10	5
10%	£11.85	−5	10	10	10	−10	15
		Project B (minimum and maximum)					
10%	£4.20	−10	10	10	10	−15	5
10%	£10.41	−10	10	10	10	−5	15

For two projects A and B, the p50 values of the cash flows are identical. Both projects have large initial capital and disposal costs. However, in project A, all the risks are in the capital costs and in project B all the risks are in the disposal costs. In each case, the risks are that the costs may vary by plus or minus 50 per cent, due to technical uncertainties.

When the cash flows are discounted for time and inflation the p50 net present value reduces from £10m to a net present value of £7.3m and the minimum and maximum net present values for the projects are £2.8m to £11.9m and £4.2m to £10.4m respectively for A and B. This shows that project A has a wider distribution of outcomes and therefore that the risk is higher.

However, if the cash flows are then further discounted for risk conventionally, the p50 net present value reduces to £6.4m, but only one value is produced and the real timing of the risk is not accounted for.

Maximum debt

Another critical measure to consider in a cash flow analysis is the maximum cumulative debt incurred. For many businesses, this is the most critical point at which a liquidity crisis can occur. If debt in the early periods increases beyond communicated expectations, investors may become nervous and may not continue to fund the venture even if it is otherwise likely to be profitable and could absorb increased debt. Investors fear the unknown most of all. If they are not aware of their true liability, they may react with scepticism to assurances when debt increases beyond previous fixed forecasts. They are then likely to become more risk-averse and so value the venture less. Used properly, risk analyses can help by communicating such risks more expertly to investors in advance and prepare them for a balanced response.

Probability of advancement

When preparing a quantitative risked cash flow model, there are some risks that may intentionally not be mapped at first. Several risks identified in the register may represent special risks to the venture that may prevent it from proceeding. Usually, these will be discrete risks, e.g. the project is stopped or not. It is important that these issues are highlighted so the risks should be identified separately. An example would be if regulatory approval were required for a project to proceed. Conditions are usually unique and involve great uncertainty that may be very difficult to resolve. A corporate view of any special risk mitigation measures required, such as corporate lobbying, should be established, together with a clear-sighted view on the probability of the outcome.

A p50 value for the project may first be established on the condition that the project proceeds, i.e. ignoring such special risks, but a second weighted p50 value can also be established, including the special risks that the project may not proceed. Simple decision trees can be drawn to demonstrate such scenarios but, as the example in Figure 5.9 shows, values derived from decision trees in this way are potentially misleading.

Fig. 5.9   Probability tree for special risks

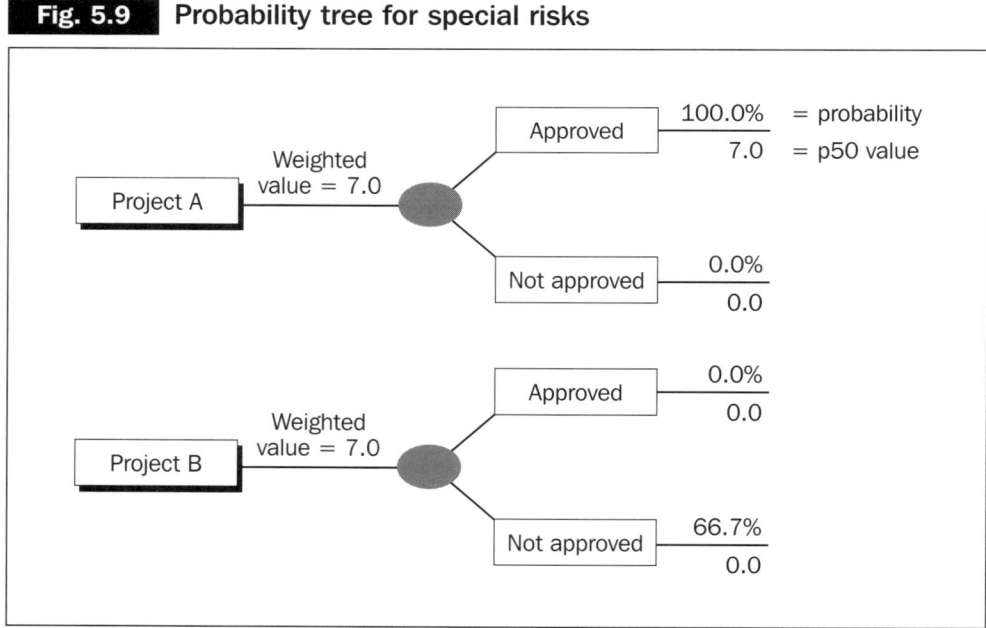

Project A has a p50 value of 7.0 (units) which is guaranteed so that the weighted value is equally 7.0 (units). In project B the p50 value is 21.0 (units) if the project proceeds but there is only an estimated one in three chance that it will proceed so the weighted value is also 7.0 (units). Therefore, the two projects A and B, with very different values and probabilities of being approved, are valued equally by this method, but if a confidence level greater than 50 per cent is applied (as we would expect), it is clear that project B would be rejected. Such possibilities are not usually so obvious and several special risks can combine to reduce the total value of a prospect, but these factors will be picked up if the risks are incorporated in the simulation model in a second all-inclusive run.

ENHANCE PROSPECT VALUES

> As an appraisal proceeds, new information will become available and opportunities will arise which should be vigorously pursued to enhance the value of the investment candidates considered.

Enlarging reward and mitigating risk

Risk and opportunity assessment is not only about valuing an option. The goal should be to maximise the opportunities available. As an appraisal proceeds, new information will become available and opportunities will arise which should be vigorously pursued to enhance the value of the investment candidates considered. There are two distinct approaches available.

- The first approach is to directly increase the expected reward from the option which may require a radical change to the whole proposal or to elements of the plans for its execution. If this is possible, new risks may be created which should be assessed.

- The second approach is to reduce the risk attached to the option. The appraisal should therefore consider the net benefits yielded by the risk reduction and mitigation measures already recorded in the risks register.

From either approach, a new distribution of results may be established which should provide a better p50 value and a narrower range of possible outcomes around that value.

Validating risk modelling and reduction

However, all new data needs to be entered into the model and validated, and unless the modifications introduce a step change in the strategy the new distribution should usually lie within the original spread of results. If results lie outside the initial ranges then something may be suspect. In this case, check the model to ensure that adequate provision has been made for all risks.

SANCTION INVESTMENTS

Verifying strategic issues

At this stage of an investment appraisal it is necessary to stand back and review the wider issues involved. The full investment appraisal will have produced a more detailed qualitative study of the issues to be considered that arise directly from the venture itself. Equally, the quantitative analysis will have properly valued and verified the significance of most of those issues. However, in the initial screening process, other wider strategic benefits may also have been qualitatively valued. To include these within the final decision criteria, they must equally have been assessed for risk and real value. This is sometimes difficult to do. For example, it may be necessary to consider the contribution that a venture may make to future business and opportunity capture, yet how that will occur might not really be understood and would entail further undefined investment.

It is not usually advisable to attempt to analyse these benefits thoroughly, but if they are relied on to sanction a venture then they must be properly evaluated. Otherwise, difficulties in defining other intangible benefits usually demonstrates that there is very high variability and risk attached to the advantages that may realistically be delivered, and they should be discounted very highly.

Nevertheless, it is useful to review the portfolio risk and reward profile for the ventures considered, based on all benefits and risks, by revisiting the screening criteria and preference model, as discussed in Chapter 4, using the updated information produced by the full investment appraisal. This will aid decision-making and selection and/or sanction of specific investments.

> **Difficulties in defining other intangible benefits usually demonstrates that there is very high variability and risk attached to the advantages that may realistically be delivered, and they should be discounted very highly.**

Setting targets and contingencies

Once a venture has been approved it is necessary to set conditions for its execution. Clear targets must be set for all aspects, including revenue, costs, time and quality aspects. The quantitative analysis will aid this process by allowing reasonable goals to be set based on a target confidence level, usually within the better half of possible outcomes.

The business must also consider the eventuality that this goal may not be achieved and allow for a 'worse' outcome by setting contingency levels at which the business or venture can remain functional. This level will usually be in the 'worse' half of possible outcomes. The contingency level will usually be more pessimistic than the sanction level, but the level required will depend on the degree of correlation of this venture with other ventures in the portfolio. If the correlation is high then higher contingencies will be required specifically for each venture, whereas if ventures are poorly correlated, contingencies may be partially shared depending on time considerations.

Setting targets and contingencies using findings from the quantitative risk analysis is shown in Figure 5.10.

Fig. 5.10 Setting targets and contingency levels

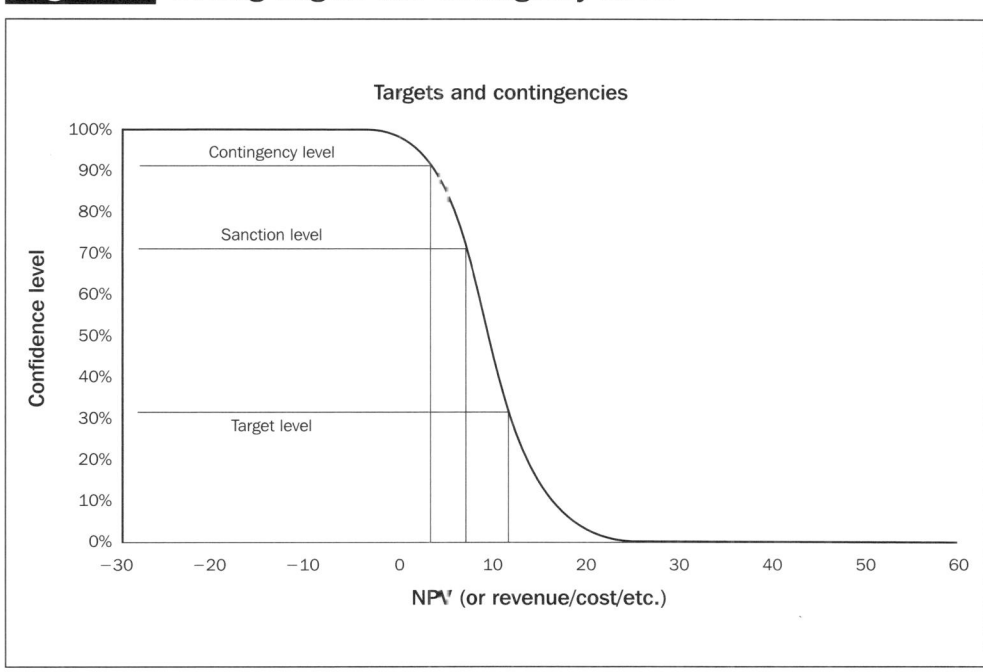

CHAPTER REVIEW

■ Full investment appraisals are best conducted for selected proposals that have already been screened against wider strategic considerations. This is the time when detailed proposals should be developed, including the identification of specific risks.

■ Record major risks in an investment uncertainty register that will provide a vehicle for risks to be formally ranked, assessed and managed, including the development of risk reduction proposals and mapping to a quantitative risk model.

■ Next, develop a risked cash flow model that will represent variables dynamically; use Monte Carlo simulation techniques to represent identified risks more completely than conventional estimating techniques. Dynamic modelling is required to allow the proper action of risks including the impact on cash flows of variable time factors. Provide inputs to the model in the form of distributions or other conditional relationships to represent the range of possible values that the risks present by mapping them from the risks register.

- At the same time correlate the variables to represent interrelationships between variables, according to an understanding of how risks are diversified or not in the business. Without this level of integrated analysis, it is not reasonable to assume that normal estimates represent good estimates of p50 values or that the full range of possible values or their probability of occurrence, and thereby the extent of risk, is correctly understood and evaluated.

- Conventionally, cash flows are discounted to derive an NPV, using a factor that represents the value of money over time, inflation and risks. This factor may be based on an organisation's WACC, but this should be adjusted to represent the actual risks presented by each unique venture. Techniques to improve the calculation of these discount factors have been demonstrated that use previous work from the strategic and screening analyses. These improved factors may be applied to the better estimates of p50 values provided by the risked cash flow model.

- Calculation of these factors remains subjective and they may only reasonably be applied to p50 values. Because other potential values within the range of outcomes offer lower or higher risk, discounting them equally for risk would under- or over-account for risk. Instead, it may be recognised that risks are inherently represented within the ranges of outcomes provided by the risked cash flow model, so that the risked cash flows need only be discounted for time and inflation. Then the value of a venture inclusive of (i.e. discounted for) risk can be determined by inspection of the range of outcomes to determine the value that meets a requisite confidence level. The confidence level must be decided by the business, according to the organisation's general tolerance for risk, the extent of risk of the particular venture (as shown by the range of outcomes against business norms) and the likely impact it may have on the total portfolio.

- Further considerations of the timing of risks, debt limitations and probability of a venture not proceeding owing to external major factors need also to be addressed against risk limitations set by the organisation. However, analysis should not focus on an initial valuation alone. Seek to improve the value of the prospect by addressing direct reward enhancement proposals along with the possible risk-reduction actions identified in the register; these, however, must themselves be reassessed for any new risks they may introduce.

- The final appraisal task is to reconsider the information provided by the full investment appraisal against the initial strategic screening criteria to ensure that all major factors have been covered. Major risks should not have been excluded. If additional subjective benefits have been excluded from the analysis they should not generally be relied upon subsequently for enhancing the perceived value if there is significant uncertainty attached to delivery of such benefits, because their value should be discounted according to the associated level of risk. If required to support a decision they should be evaluated more fully.

- Remember that, when sanctioning an investment, targets and contingencies may be more realistically set for the appraisal, using the improved outputs from the analysis as they provide varying confidence levels of different outcomes being achieved. These clear targets and the detailed information on objectives and risks provided by the appraisal should now be formally passed on to the execution teams. These issues are covered further in the next chapter.

6

Stage 4: Development and planning

INTRODUCTION

An investment scheme which proceeds to project Development and Planning (D&P) has been assessed as viable and sufficiently interesting to justify substantial investment. It will have received either full investment sanction, or partial sanction to cover the D&P stage, depending on the extent of uncertainty still outstanding. In the first case the substance of D&P work is preparatory in nature, with the assumption that implementation will follow. In the second, it is both investigative and preparatory, with an open question as to whether or not it will be implemented.

This chapter covers the following aspects of development and planning:

- *Preparing to deliver value* Attention turns to the influence of whether or not there has been full investment sanction on D&P objectives. The discussion emphasises the scale of commitments and rewards influenced, if not largely determined, by the effort invested in D&P, and identifies three foci for D&P work. D&P objectives are grouped by area of D&P work focus. They are described, with distinctions between those applicable to investment justification and those involving preparation for delivery.

- *Achieving development and planning objectives* Presentation includes guidelines for achieving D&P objectives. Some concern prerequisites for carrying out D&P work, whilst others relate to steps during that work. Particular attention is given to the management and use of the uncertainty register and how reviews can give early warnings of actions required. Finally, there is discussion of the use of a project masterplan which provides the focus for much risk management.

- *Aligning responsibilities for risk* The implications are examined when responsibility does not reside with the parties who are best able to manage the risk. This is particularly relevant for achieving the intended outcome in negotiations.

- *Final investment appraisal* Discussion identifies requisites of the review that represents the last barrier to inappropriate investment.

- *Authorising implementation* Preparations for handover to the implementation team include measures to ensure that there are no inconsistencies between the bases for full investment sanction and the scope and objectives inherited by implementation management. These measures are stated, and attention is given to the matter of setting targets and contingencies.

FOCUS AND OBJECTIVES

Preparing to deliver value

Levering delivery with preparation

Having successfully passed through full investment appraisal and emerged as an investment perceived as both viable and desirable, the scheme now enters the execution phase. Those sanctioning capital development must now resist both the overwhelming temptation or the compelling pressure to rush headlong into asset delivery once there has been a decision in principle to proceed with a scheme. It will be largely their responsibility to ensure that adequate time and resources are directed at developing their scheme design and planning its implementation.

> The quality of the preparatory work will have a profound influence on the value for money delivered in implementation.

Project D&P may embrace all the preparatory work for full implementation. This is probably the case where full investment appraisal has presented a particularly strong case for the venture, with insufficient risk exposure to impose conditions on full investment sanction. Alternatively, the results of D&P, themselves, may determine whether or not the scheme will win full commitment. Often the scale of resources expended for these preparations will be an order of magnitude less than that of the subsequent implementation work, but the quality of the preparatory work will have a profound influence on the value for money delivered in implementation.

Whether D&P are undertaken solely as preparations for implementation, or are also to determine if full investment should go ahead, will influence the specific objectives of work during this stage. Figure 6.1 illustrates the distinction.

Focus for preparations

All the effort consumed during project development and planning can be divided into three areas of focus (*see* Table 6.1):

1 Validation of, and refinements to, design of the investment scheme ('What should be our destination?');

2 Preliminary planning of scheme implementation ('How should we get there?');

3 Management of D&P stage work ('Let's come up with the answers, within the time and resources available').

Fig. 6.1 Multiple D&P objectives

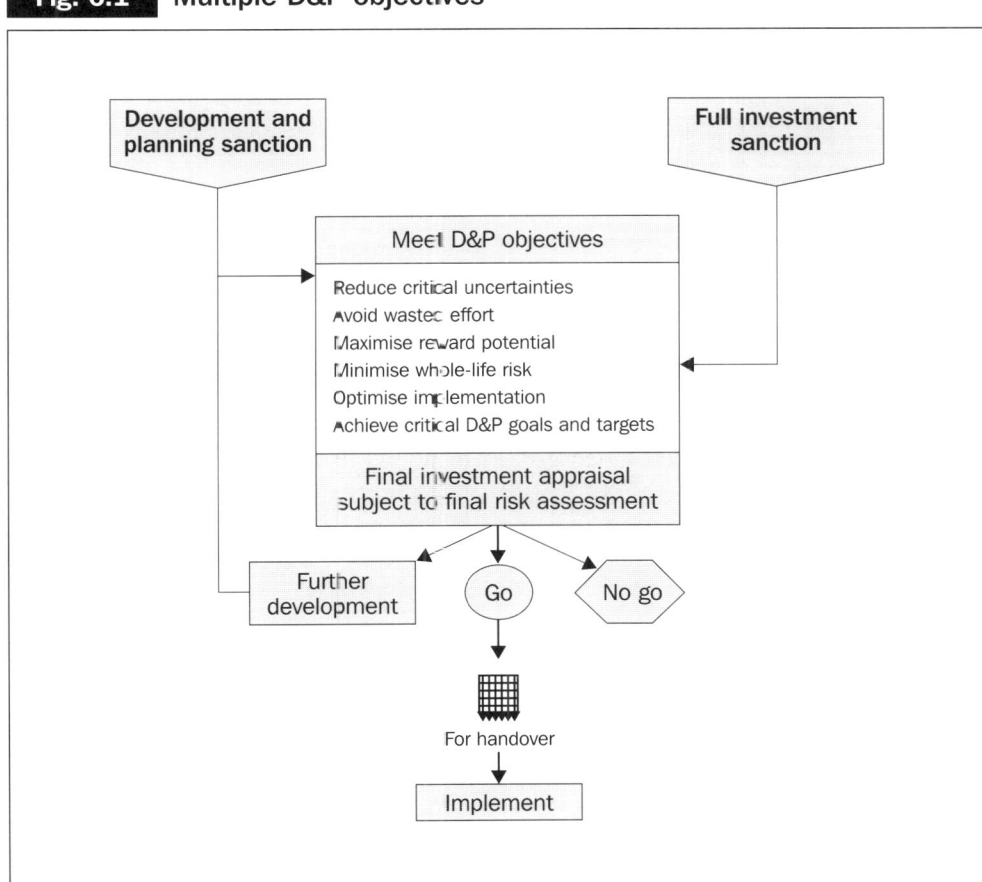

The six objectives of project development and planning shown in Figure 6.1 are grouped below according to these areas of focus.

Table 6.1 Activities to meet project D&P objectives

Focus	Project D&P stage objectives	Typical stage activities
Validation of and refinement to design of investment scheme	Reduce critical uncertainties	■ Market analysis ■ Value analysis ■ Research ■ Design development ■ Prototyping ■ Piloting
	Avoid wasted effort	■ Investment reviews ■ Value analysis reviews
	Maximise reward potential and minimise implementation, operation and divestment stage risks	■ Execution of all planned actions to enhance prospects ■ Monitoring and control of actions ■ Reiterative value analysis

Focus	Project D&P stage objectives	Typical stage activities
		■ Testing and selection of design solutions ■ Reiteration of uncertainty management process to identify and plan new actions to enhance prospects ■ Development of commercial strategy.
Preliminary planning of scheme implementation	Optimise implementation strategy and plan	■ Testing and selection of implementation options ■ Product breakdown structure ■ Organisation breakdown structure ■ Work breakdown structure ■ Cost breakdown structure ■ Project management plan with implementation master plan and schedule ■ Cost management plan with implementation budget ■ Risk management plans ■ Value, quality, resource, configuration and other management plans, as appropriate ■ Contracting strategy ■ Financing plan ■ Tender specifications ■ Tender evaluations ■ Contract regulations
Management of D&P stage work	Achieve critical D&P goals and targets	■ Project management of stage

Design of investment scheme

Reduce critical uncertainties

Where authorisation has fallen short of full investment sanction, the first objective of the D&P stage is to develop knowledge relating to those uncertainties which prevented an unconditional go-ahead for the scheme.

Avoid wasted effort

There should be sufficient flexibility to abort a scheme at any point during D&P where review of the investment case suggests that a final 'no go' decision can be taken. Even early results from measures to reduce uncertainty should, at D&P management's discretion, constitute a basis for review of the investment. This review very probably will include a quantitative update of the investment model as well as a qualitative review of the uncertainty register.

Maximise reward potential

Identification and analysis of opportunities for enhancing investment reward and the development of strategies and actioning of measures to capture and exploit those opportunities should be ongoing throughout D&P. The focus, understandably, is on decisions that affect the performance of an investment through its whole life.

Minimise implementation, operations and divestment risk

D&P work reduces adverse influences in general, and risks from change in particular, during the subsequent implementation, operations and divestment stages.

The activities comprising risk management during this stage are inseparable from the ongoing process of identifying, capturing and exploiting opportunities to enhance reward over the whole life of the investment. They merely reflect a different emphasis. Instead of increasing the likelihood of fortuitous events and circumstances and maximising beneficial impacts, management is reducing the likelihood of unfavourable events and circumstances and is also minimising their impacts.

Preliminary planning of scheme implementation

Optimise implementation strategy and plan

Proper planning introduces structure, dimensions and the ability to influence uncertainty for the work ahead. Its effect is to:

- clarify uncertainties by defining their boundaries;
- reduce uncertainties through definition of work content, task interrelationships, resource requirements and external dependencies;
- identify and thus help to prevent fruitless pursuit of unachievable goals and targets;
- maximise potential for reward and minimise risks, through quantifying cost/benefit trade-offs and by testing implementation options for their effects on the whole life of the investment as well as on implementation performance;

> There should be sufficient flexibility to abort a scheme at any point during D&P.

123

■ establish strategies and actions, to be incorporated into the implementation plan and budget, which realise opportunities and reduce risks.

Project D&P management

Achieve critical D&P goals and targets

It is important to appreciate that D&P constitutes a project in its own right. This stage entails significant expenditure of funds and use of valuable resources often in short supply and great demand. Its success in delivering the benefits within the D&P budget and schedule targets demands the use of effective project management disciplines and skills.

The project D&P stage may itself be broken into successive steps, each requiring its own sanction to proceed. Incremental D&P serves as a means of limiting commitment to a level appropriate to the extent of uncertainty and risk at each stage. One added refinement that is increasingly employed is to combine the incremental stages with an element of competition between projects up to, but not including, full development. The purpose of this refined approach is to improve value for money through extended effort and expenditure at the front end of procurement/execution. Prominent examples of this refined approach occur in the development of complex military systems involving state-of-the-art technology applications.

A general shortfall in quality of the deliverables from D&P can impair the quality of a 'go/no go' decision on full implementation. It can also undermine the realism of implementation goals and the efficiency of implementation work. An overrun in cost for D&P, if incurred to protect the quality of its deliverables, is probably of little significance if the investment proceeds. On the other hand, an overrun in the D&P schedule can lead to lost opportunities in a highly competitive market. As a result, buyers should beware. Tenders masking inadequate D&P are far more common than tenders submitted after the required date!

GUIDELINES FOR ACHIEVING PROJECT D&P OBJECTIVES

Confirm investment and D&P objectives and work scopes

No one would argue against the principle that every project should commence with a confirmation of its approval and communication to all involved of its objectives and work scopes. Yet this principle is so often overlooked in the excitement of a project kick-off. Assumption too often replaces confirmation in the rush to get on with 'real work'. Unfortunately, this often results in as many different individual assumptions of objectives and work scope as there are project participants. A lack of common focus and coordinated effort are thus pre-ordained. Confirmation and communication of specific objectives and work scopes must, therefore, be explicit.

Upon handover of a successful candidate investment scheme from full investment appraisal, key members of the management team from that earlier stage and business management representatives should join with the new D&P stage management team in the definition of agreed objectives, scopes and targets relating to the work they are about to undertake. The start of D&P gives key participants of the new team an important opportunity to:

- clarify and confirm with business management the overall investment objectives and scope;
- clarify and agree, with business management and amongst themselves, the stage objectives, work scope and any specific targets, including schedule and budget allocations.

> Assumption too often replaces confirmation in the rush to get on with 'real work'. Confirmation and communication of specific objectives and work scopes must, therefore, be explicit.

Work to a risk management plan

The management of uncertainty and its influences is fundamental to the achievement of all the confirmed objectives for the project development and planning stage. It touches all aspects of preparation for the implementation stage and enlists the participation of all the functions involved in evaluating and executing an investment scheme. As such, it is a major contributor to coherent and coordinated preparatory efforts across the organisation.

Unlike most project D&P stage plans, one for risk management needs to distinguish between management of the uncertainties affecting achievement of objectives for the stage concerned (implementation) and management of uncertainties which influence achievement of whole-life investment objectives.

> The risk management plan should define the process, organisation and procedures for supporting stage management with reviews, analysis, actioning, monitoring and reporting of all matters relating to uncertainty and risk.

The tasks undertaken to achieve development and planning objectives involve all the steps in the reiterative risk management process described in Chapter 2. The risk management plan should define the process, organisation and procedures for supporting stage management with reviews, analysis, actioning, monitoring and reporting of all matters relating to uncertainty and risk. The ongoing review and analysis work provides both a framework and an impetus for active cross-functional participation throughout the management and execution of project development and planning.

The risk management plan should specify any vehicles for qualitative analysis, including, as a minimum, the investment uncertainty register developed during full investment appraisal, which will be maintained throughout project D&P and thereafter as an essential management support tool. In the same way, the plan should specify the risk model(s) to be used for quantitative analysis, including as a minimum the investment risk model(s) inherited from the full investment appraisal stage. The evolution of models also needs to be controlled and documented, to ensure that changes can be traced. People are surprised how often they need to return to earlier analyses as circumstances alter – not to mention the requirement to explain changes to others.

Review and action the uncertainty register

The new D&P management team will have convened with representatives of business management and the previous full investment appraisal stage team, for the purpose of confirming objectives and scopes. This meeting gives them the added opportunity whilst in open forum to:

- review the investment uncertainty register for the project, including the validity of assumptions carried over from the previous stage;
- assign responsibilities amongst the team for D&P stage actions to reduce uncertainties or risks or to enhance opportunities.

Occasionally, in a particularly extensive, complex and costly D&P stage, the management team will choose to develop and use an additional lower-level uncertainty register as described in Chapter 2. This is an effective way of managing those uncertainties which specifically influence D&P work and objectives as distinct from overall investment objectives.

Subsequent meetings of the D&P team will follow up the regular monitoring of progress in uncertainty and risk reduction and opportunity enhancement with:

- accountability of individuals responsible for agreed actions;
- intervention where actual progress falls short of that planned for critical uncertainties.

Without executive follow-up, the process delivers little or no value.

Figure 6.2 illustrates an example of progress in investment design where risk reduction was carried out on a complex electronics system investment during the project development and planning stage.

Fig. 6.2 Example of D&P progress in managing the risk inventory

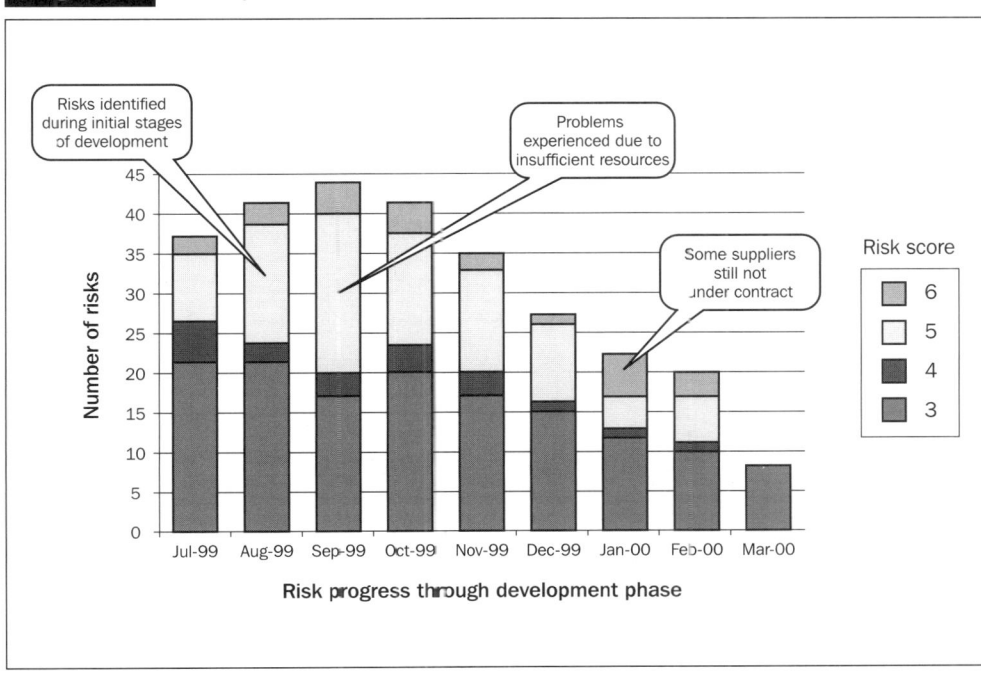

Fill critical knowledge gaps to reduce uncertainties

Uncertainties with influences which are critical to investment success, like those of market demand and competitor pricing, might be external to the managed activities of the investment. Other critical uncertainties might relate to, or arise from, investment work content. Examples of the latter are uncertainty with respect to design productivity or operational logistics costs, and future results from prototype testing. Whatever the case, the risk management process should initiate specific measures to fill knowledge gaps and reduce the uncertainties in the uncertainty register as much and as early as possible during project development and planning.

Reduced uncertainty does not always improve the outlook (as has been explained in Chapter 2). On the contrary, it may reinforce worst expectations or, at the very least, provide insufficient justification for further pursuit of the scheme. Aggressive management use of the uncertainty register ensures unsuitable schemes are ruled out as early as possible.

This happens regularly in the energy industry, where anticipations of recoverable reserves are disappointed during the course of exploration and assessment. In the fast-moving electronics industries new-technology substitutes can produce collapse in markets for products based on existing technology. More generally, political and global economic changes exert profound effects on market expectations, planned capital and operating costs and forecasts of investment value.

The risk management process should initiate specific measures to fill knowledge gaps and reduce the uncertainties in the uncertainty register as much and as early as possible during project development and planning.

Uncertainty reduction implies quantitative findings, and most probably achievement of this objective will require quantitative analysis updates of the investment risk model developed during full investment appraisal and supporting sub-models, based on critical knowledge as it is acquired. The results will indicate the extent of further uncertainty reduction required if this is not already apparent.

Review for early warning

During D&P avoidance of wasted effort comes through early warning. Early warning is the result of timely reviews of progress in the reduction of critical uncertainties. These reviews should not be confined to periodic updates if new information reveals the need for more urgency.

Research by one tour business operator into product opportunities based on consumer demand revealed that current data on consumer behaviour was becoming out of date even as it was being compiled, owing to the technical revolution in electronic commerce and direct buying. Thus research efforts to reduce one area of uncertainty relating to product-based demand had identified a new area of uncertainty.

In this case, routine review of the uncertainty register led to the formal identification and actioning of the new uncertainty on a prioritised basis. The resultant early shift in emphasis meant that more effort was fruitfully directed to customer information, booking access and convenience, and that less effort was spent on aspects of product offerings that were of diminishing importance.

Integrate with value management and other disciplines

The natural links between uncertainty management and value management are extensive and call for a complete integration of the two. Every decision based on value criteria will be accompanied by uncertainties which attach to the financial and other measures of costs and benefits. Without the totally integrated management of value and uncertainty, neither will fully deliver its potential benefits. A practical approach is to:

- incorporate identified value objectives as a subset of investment/business objectives within the risk management process;
- enhance the functional analysis which underpins the analysis and management of value by depicting the influence of uncertainty on benefits and costs for alternative solution designs.

The embedding of value management elements within risk management as inseparable aspects of maximising reward potential and minimising risk is particularly appropriate to the project D&P stage since:

> **The natural links between uncertainty management and value management are extensive and call for a complete integration of the two.**

- the potential gains from both risk management and value management are dramatically higher than they are later in implementation;

- options for investment and implementation design solutions have become sufficiently defined to be described in dimensions of time and through-life cost as well as in measures of income and other value terms.

The management plans for disciplines such as Health and Safety, Environment, Configuration Management, Change Control Management, Quality Management, and ARM (Availability/Reliability/Maintainability) studies also need mechanisms for coordination where they have implications for investment or business risk or opportunity. The natural vehicles for effecting it are the uncertainty registers, where provision can be made for the flow of information on critical risks from the register used for each other type of risk to the investment and/or business uncertainty register, as appropriate.

Design and plan scheme implementation

To a great extent the quality of a project's planning will determine the quality of its implementation. In designing and planning the implementation stage, attention turns from what implementation should deliver to how it will be delivered. The accommodation of uncertainty, risk and opportunity in designing and planning the implementation stage profoundly influences the reliability, effectiveness and general quality of the planning.

The implementation masterplan provides the logic structure and initial estimating dimensions for any implementation schedule risk analysis or schedule-driven cost or investment risk analysis. If the masterplan is missing or deficient, analysis and forecasting incorporating the influence of time uncertainties lack an acceptable foundation. Its importance to the setting of challenging but achievable implementation targets and programmes through the use of uncertainty modelling cannot be overstated.

An implementation master plan must be prepared which is more than simply an unresourced bar graph of implementation activities neatly phased to produce the desired end date required. At the very least, it needs to be a sequence of project implementation activities defined by fundamental interdependencies and supportable work practice. Its form is that of the project activity network.

Bar graphs and schedule forecasts, to warrant credibility, must be the products of:

- the combined contributions of all functions participating in implementation;

- the constraints, other interdependencies and planned work sequence defined in the masterplan activity network;

- estimates of activity durations which reflect resource availabilities.

An implementation master plan must be prepared which is more than simply an unresourced bar graph of implementation activities neatly phased to produce the desired end date required.

129

Otherwise they are meaningless pictures capable of manipulation at will to serve a presenter's purpose.

There is no formula for the level of detail required in an implementation master plan. In general, it should carry sufficient definition to reflect major interdependencies between activities and key interfaces between participants, yet be manageable enough to test alternative implementation options and risk/reward sharing proposals in a responsive manner. An experienced view is that an implementation master plan should contain several hundred activities at the most. More common during project development and planning are implementation master plans of 50 to 150 activities.

RISK RESPONSIBILITY ALIGNMENT

The principle of allocating management of a risk to the party best equipped and positioned to control or at least influence it is well established in project risk management. Such principles should be applied more often to commercial strategies for implementation.

- Management responsibility might be appropriately allocated, but ownership of risk burdens and potential rewards should also reside with parties best able to influence or control the risks and opportunities.
- Distribution of potential reward should be equitable when compared with respective risk exposures.
- Risk- and gain-sharing schemes should lead to alignment of participants' objectives, thus minimising conflict of interests.

Seriously flawed commercial strategies can be avoided by subjecting proposed strategies to simple qualitative analyses of the alignment between risks and responsibilities and their suitability for dealing with identified uncertainties and related risks and opportunities. Figure 6.3 illustrates a quick visual check for misalignments between ownership of consequence ('Party impacted') and management responsibility ('Responsible party') for a contractor and his customer. Hatched areas signify serious misalignments which can be depended upon to serve at least one, and probably both, parties poorly, leading to contention and acrimonious conflict in the process. Variations on format can be used to similarly check alignments between management responsibility and ability to control.

Seriously flawed commercial strategies can be avoided by subjecting proposed strategies to simple qualitative analyses of the alignment between risks and responsibilities

Fig. 6.3 Example of alignment check between management responsibility and ownership of consequences

ID	Risk title	Responsible party	Party impacted	Score
9	Programme plan uncertainties	Project	Project	6
20A	Data migration tools and process	Project	Project	5
23	Systems architecture uncertainties	Project	Project	4
2	Requirements not correctly identified and bought into	Project	Project	3
20B	Data migration impact on deployment	Project	Project	3
21	Functional acceptance uncertainties	Project	Project	3
24	Continued development of legacy systems	Project	Project	1
34	Dependency on management of change infrastructure projects	Corporate	Project	6
6	Project sources	Corporate	Project	6
13	Roles and responsibilities	Corporate	Project	3
12	Scope containment	Project/Customer	Project	2
19	Legacy systems year 2000 compliance	Project/Customer	Project	2
15	Customer expectations/contract ambiguity	Project/Customer	Project	6
8	Relationship with client organisation	Corporate/Customer	Project	5
16	Dependency on customer global systems	Customer	Project	6
7	Provision of customer resources in support of the project	Customer	Project	2
32	Transition scope and resources	Project	Customer	2
23A	Ability to meet service level targets	Project	Customer	5
28	Roll-out uncertainties	Project/Customer	Project/Customer	3

This approach has an immediate benefit when used in negotiations with contractors and the evaluation of tenders. Superior knowledge contributes to superior strength, and risk management frequently demonstrates its ability to give a critical edge to the party who can use it most effectively, by adding value to the following commercial activities:

■ negotiation of contractual targets and risk and reward sharing mechanisms, with associated 'floors' and 'ceilings' on shared amounts;

- development of tender specifications for
  - uncertainty analysis required to substantiate depth of knowledge behind tendered solutions, validity of those solutions and promises of time, cost and technical performance
  - risk management plans to be submitted with tenders for application throughout contract work;
- evaluation of tenders with respect to:
  - tenderer's appreciation of uncertainties, their influence and solutions for their management
  - credibility of promised time, cost and technical performance
  - effectiveness of proposed risk management organisation, procedures and techniques.

Quantitative modelling of uncertainty is especially useful in testing specific proposed risk and gain-sharing formulae for their equitability under various scenarios, including foreseeable extreme circumstances. Its use is increasingly common in alliance contracting in the oil and gas industry and should be considered for any negotiation of risk and gain-sharing arrangements. Selection of appropriate modelling skills and tools is of paramount importance for such support.

Risk modelling of tenders provides a frequently used and powerful means of challenging or verifying achievability of proposed work schedules, budgets and resource plans for implementation stage work. It pays great dividends for the effort expended and is highly recommended. Even retrospective modelling of uncertainty that existed at the time of contract award has been employed on occasion, to discredit unjustified claims arising from large defence procurement contracts where out-turn costs ended up being multiples of contracted prices. Unfortunately, such demonstrations of the unachieveability of contracted programmes and targets, when conducted after the event, highlight what could have been prevented by better scrutiny – before the event!

FINAL INVESTMENT APPRAISAL

Development and planning may or may not have run its full course with authorisation for implementation dependent on its results. At whatever point it occurs during the stage, final review of the business case with its risks and potential delivered value and other rewards provides a last chance to prevent an inappropriate investment.

It is vital that this review:

- takes into account the effects, on the business case, of any major changes to the assumptions used in full investment appraisal, that might have taken place during development and planning;

- takes into account any major changes to investment or business objectives which might have occurred;
- updates and analyses the investment risk model to test ranges and confidence levels for investment performance;
- scrutinises all the implementation stage planning, with its proposed schedules and budgets.

The culmination of this final review is the 'go/no go' decision for implementation.

AUTHORISING IMPLEMENTATION

Preparing for handover

With a 'go' decision for implementation, the scheme approaches the point where handover will take place. At this point:

- business and investment objectives and priorities should be re-affirmed;
- any changes required by the sanctioning authority (business management) to implementation planning need to be agreed with the implementation stage management team;
- implementation schedules and capital budgets must be ratified and contingency levels established.

Quantitative uncertainty analysis will aid the process of setting challenging but reasonable goals based on target confidence levels.

Setting targets and contingencies

Once the scheme has been approved, it is necessary to set conditions for its execution. Clear targets must be set for various aspects, including revenue, costs, time and quality. Quantitative uncertainty analysis will aid the process of setting challenging but reasonable goals based on target confidence levels which should usually be within the better half of possible outcomes.

At the same time the business must also consider the eventuality that these goals may not be achieved and allow for a worse outcome by setting contingency levels at which the business or investment scheme can remain viable. The contingency levels will usually be more pessimistic than the sanction levels. The actual levels required will depend on the degree of correlation of this scheme with other ventures in the business portfolio. If the correlation is high, then higher contingencies will be required specifically for each venture, whereas if ventures have little correlation, contingencies may be partially shared depending on time considerations.

Fig. 6.4 Setting targets and contingency levels

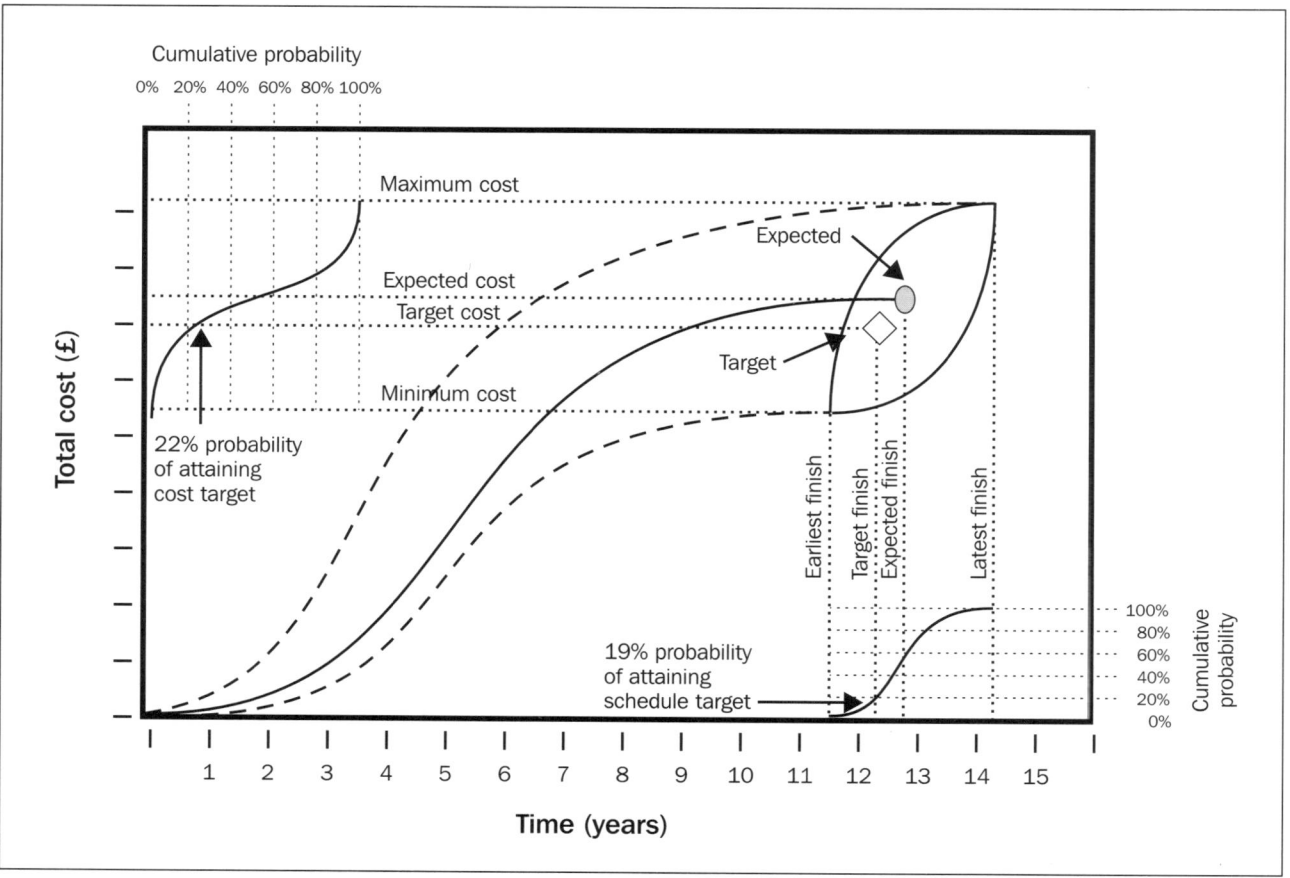

Figure 6.4 illustrates the use of similar quantitative modelling to set challenging planning and budget targets for implementation. The 'cat's eye' represents the universe of possible time and cost performance. Analytically, this would be defined by a scatter diagram produced from a Monte Carlo simulation integrating time and cost. The targets in this case are more ambitious than average expectancy in respect of both time and cost. It could be argued that the time target is challenging to the extent of being unrealistic. As a tasking target imposed on an implementation team, it could disincentivise and prove to be counter-productive.

CHAPTER REVIEW

- Uncertainty management's contribution to development and planning aims at 'getting it right' prior to major investment.

- Its potential benefits from proactive discovery and management of major uncertainty issues are greater than at any subsequent stage.

■ Confirmation of investment and D&P scopes and objectives is an important bridge between full investment appraisal and D&P to ensure continuity of thinking up to date in focus, and a reliable reference for risk and opportunity.

■ Uncertainty registers at various levels of management should be used to provide upward communication of information on uncertainties relevant to higher level objectives, downward communication of higher level priorities, and the basis for ensuring that actions are carried out.

■ Reduction of major uncertainties by early focus on critical knowledge gaps is the first step in avoiding wasted effort in pursuit of unviable schemes.

■ Frequent reviews of the investment uncertainty register and investment risk model provide the early warnings that can enable management to re-direct development resources and efforts as emerging knowledge changes outlooks and priorities.

■ The greatest combined benefits from uncertainty management and value management are to be realised during the D&P stage through integration of the two disciplines.

■ Implementation master plans and budgets need to be the end products of rigorous qualitative and quantitative analysis of uncertainties.

■ The project risk management principle of allocating management of risk to the party best able to influence it needs to be applied and extended in developing commercial strategies for implementation.

■ Final investment appraisal affords the last opportunity to assess the influences of uncertainty on implementation and whole-life investment performance prospects before a 'go/no go' decision on full investment.

Stage 5: Implementation

INTRODUCTION

The challenge presented to management during implementation is to make decisions which actively look over the whole life-cycle of the investment. Risk management processes provide a proven approach for protecting anticipated investment returns and delivery of business goals.

This final chapter draws upon lessons from project risk management to offer guidelines for achieving this protection. Specific reference is made to projects involving third parties, where differences in objectives are notorious for introducing difficulties, and can be a major cause of projects failing to achieve their targets. Topics covered include the following:

- *Achieving investment and business objectives in implementation*   Objectives are identified for the implementation stage, followed by a brief explanation of how differences in vested interest and perspectives lead to mismatched objectives. Discussion then proposes principles that offer the means of ensuring that investment and business priorities predominate throughout implementation.

- *Implementation risk management*   Coverage offers guidelines for achieving the stage objectives. It explains the need for the risk management process to be given a large degree of independence since it has to be able to handle conflicts of interest. The risk register is used to manage information and, in practice, there will be a hierarchy of risk registers equating to the needs of different levels of management. These qualitative registers are supported by quantitative models. Much of the emphasis is on the integration of risk management with project management and how progress is demonstrated towards targets.

- *Pre-operations investment review*   This section stresses the importance of a review to ensure the currency of the assumptions and business objectives on which operations strategies, plans and budgets are based, and the reasonableness of investment expectations in light of any changes which have occurred during implementation.

- *Handover to operations*   The latest investment review is proposed as a means of fine tuning operations stage objectives, plans, and budget and other targets prior to handover.

Risk management processes provide a proven approach for protecting anticipated investment returns and delivery of business goals.

ACHIEVING INVESTMENT AND BUSINESS OBJECTIVES IN IMPLEMENTATION

Investment and business objectives

Much of the possible reduction of uncertainty and investment risk and enhancement of reward potential will have taken place by completion of the project development and planning stage. With the start of implementation, emphasis changes gradually:

- from risk reduction toward risk containment;

- from opportunity enhancement toward preservation of potential value and investment return.

As long as significant uncertainty remains, initiatives and measures will strive to achieve the best possible results. Nevertheless, relative to the gains made up through project D&P, the deliverable whole-life benefits from risk management during implementation are likely to be less dramatic as work progresses.

The investment scheme has now passed into the stage of investment execution. Since the early 1970s, project risk management has evolved as a practical management discipline to deal with the downside of project uncertainties. A growing number of books, industry- and profession-based guidelines and courses are available to implementation ('project') managers to familiarise them with the processes, alternative practices and available techniques for project risk management.

The effective continuation of risk management through implementation will resemble established project risk management practice, but with two notable exceptions:

- emphasis on capturing and exploiting remaining and emergent opportunities to maximise reward, as well as that placed on minimising risk;

- the protection of whole-life investment and business objectives, through the 'communication between registers' and through the business-driven organisation of risk management.

Divergent objectives

Implementation is the first stage in the investment cycle where objectives are apt to conflict substantially with the interests of operations management in particular respects, and with investment and business objectives in general.

A specific situation where conflicts arise is when one organisation implements the investment while another operates it. For example, an information systems department might provide a user department with a computer application, or a contractor might provide a customer with a facility. Where implementation work content is wholly or largely in the hands of contractors, the divergence of interests takes on a commercial dimension and edge.

To an owner taking delivery of an asset at the end of implementation, whole life extends through the operational life of that asset until he divests himself of it. From the implementation contractor's standpoint, investment whole life is apt to end upon either delivery or on receipt of his final payment. Without a major stake in his customer's whole-life investment performance, his interests will be necessarily short term and geared largely to containing unrecoverable costs and project schedule. Incentives and penalties attached to quality, functionality, technical performance, reliability and any other deliverable attributes that influence whole-life value to the owner may temper, but will not eliminate, the conflict of interest.

Bearing in mind these different perspectives as well as the possible conflicts of interest between the stages and levels of investment management, it is worth considering the first questions that should always be asked in project risk management: Risk to whom? From whose perspective are uncertainty and its influences being addressed? Depending on which perspective that is, the objectives of risk management during implementation will be to:

- maximise investment reward (value and return) potential;

- minimise operations and whole-life risk;

- complete implementation deliverables to specification, to schedule and to budget.

Those parties responsible for realising investment and business goals (e.g. asset owners) will be concerned primarily with the first two objectives. They will involve themselves with the third only to the extent that it affects achievement of the other two objectives. Managers responsible for achieving implementation targets only (e.g. implementation/project managers and sub-project managers) will be focused on the third objective. Contractors will pursue all three objectives, except that investment and whole life for them will be confined to the scopes and durations of their respective contracts.

The challenge for those accountable for investment and business performance will be to ensure that their broader priorities predominate in key decisions within implementation management. They can achieve this by means of:

- contractual or internal allocations of management responsibility which align well with ability to influence, if not control;

> The challenge for those accountable for investment and business performance will be to ensure that their broader priorities predominate in key decisions within implementation management.

- contractual or internal incentives which align well with investment and business objectives;

- superior knowledge of significant uncertainties, solutions for managing them and their influences and progress toward that end.

IMPLEMENTATION RISK MANAGEMENT

Confirm investment and implementation objectives and scopes

From the project development and planning stage onwards, the execution of a selected investment scheme, and the substantial commitments that that entails, make it essential to capture as early as possible any emergent circumstances or business re-thinking that might materially influence:

- investment strategies, and hence a particular scheme's fit with those strategies;

- assumptions underpinning investment or scheme execution strategies;

- objectives or scope for a particular scheme.

The formal convening of business and stage managements, not only at commencement of the implementation stage, but also at subsequent key commitment points, should be a matter of course to ensure the capture of such changes and their implications to the work ahead. As at the beginning of the project development and planning stage, confirmation and communication must replace personal assumptions on the matters of objectives and scope.

Implementation stage management will have participated alongside the D&P team throughout implementation planning preparations, including the definition of agreed objectives and scope, and targets for project delivery work. At the start of the implementation stage, all personnel with key responsibilities within the implementation team should convene to:

- clarify and confirm, in collaboration with representatives from business management, overall investment objectives and scope;

- clarify and agree amongst themselves the implementation objectives and work scope, specific targets, including schedule and budget allocations within the stage work scope;

- clarify the project management organisation with its assignments and delineations of authority and responsibility.

Organise for risk management

The risk management plan for implementation, more than for any other stage, needs to have spelled out clearly and in organisational terms the distinction between custodianship of the management process and ownership of the application. That distinction can draw upon two principles:

- the risk management process must serve those responsible for achieving objectives threatened or otherwise affected by uncertainty;
- the integrity of the process should be, and should be seen to be, in the hands of an independent party with no vested interest in the analytical findings or forecasts, other than concern for their reliability.

These principles should be satisfied by organisational arrangements for risk management at every level of management during the implementation process, and overall management of the risk management process must have single-point accountability which represents the highest level of business and investment authority in the organisation. The management team charged with delivering an asset to schedule and to budget will have one agenda. The team that will inherit the asset and have to operate it throughout its life will have another. Overall custodianship of the risk management process may be the only safeguard to ensure that key implementation decisions are based on consideration of business and investment whole-life trade-offs.

There are alternative organisational solutions:

- an independent overall custodian manages business, investment and implementation-level risk management systems with ultimate accountability to business management;
- business management nominates an independent custodian to look after its own business and investment-level risk management system, but requires implementation management to use an independent custodian of its choosing for overall management of the implementation-level system, with 'open book' reporting and access at all implementation levels.

Both approaches ensure an independent view of implementation risk with full investor access to implementation analysis and reporting. Both can accommodate direct support to the implementation team in its management of uncertainty, risk and opportunity at all levels. The second approach might better suit situations where implementation management resides with an external contractor.

Whichever organisational solution is used, reporting should be direct to the management supported by risk management, and not to project/information services functions. Without that direct support to decision-makers, reliability of information delivered and responsiveness to management needs can be too easily subordinated to other interests.

The risk management plan

We have already emphasised the natural tendency for implementation ('project') management to focus on its contracted commitments rather than on overall investment or business objectives. Because of this tendency, the procedures prescribed by the risk management plan for the management of uncertainty and its influences during the implementation stage must call for:

- maintenance of separate business, investment and implementation uncertainty registers reflecting business, investment whole-life and implementation stage objectives, respectively;

- upward flow of register information on uncertainties and associated risks and opportunities which influence achievability of higher-level objectives (i.e. sub-project level to implementation level, to investment level, and thence to business level, as appropriate);

- communication of overriding priorities to lower management levels through the registers (i.e. business level to investment level, to implementation level, and thence to sub-project level, as appropriate).

In the case of contractors and subcontractors, the responsibility to maintain their own uncertainty registers and communicate information may be a contractual requirement.

As for implementation masterplans, there is no formula for size of uncertainty registers. Repeated experience suggests that attempts to monitor, analyse, report on and manage appreciably more than 40 to 50 key uncertainties with their associated risks and opportunities tend to become counter-productive. The discipline loses its focus, and management perceives itself as spending too much effort feeding an information and analysis system. In addition, populating registers only with uncertainties that generate significant risk or opportunity, and excluding problems that are significant intrinsic to the work to be done, is guaranteed to help contain the size of each register. For a given management level and work scope, the risks and opportunities should be significant at that level and not repeating those belonging to lower management levels.

Table 7.1 is an example of a contractor's internal uncertainty register summary list for asset management. Whereas a register for a private finance initiative investment might cover both implementation and operations stages, this one encompasses the operations stage only. The scores in this case combine the highest grade of impact (cost, income, strategic) with the likelihood, for application of a scoring algorithm. No relative weightings have been given to cost, income and strategic impacts.

Table 7.1 Top 10 uncertainty issues for an asset management programme

Risk ID	Risk title	Likelihood	Cost impact	Income impact	Strat. impact	Score
01	Inability to man job	High	Med	High	Low	6
04	Technical resistance to innovation	High	High	High	Low	6
09	Owner inability to deliver expertise/systems/data	High	High	Med	Med	6
10	Contractor inability to deliver expertise/systems/data	High	High	High	Med	6
11	Contract failure to anticipate growth issues	High	High	High	High	6
06	Failure to seek opportunities at tactical level	Med	High	High	Low	5
26	Failure to manage transition	Med	Med	High	Low	5
03	Lack of contractor continuity at senior operational levels	High	Low	Med	Low	5
07	Early economic barriers to incremental production improvements	High	Med	Med	Low	5
25	Year 2000 failures	High	Med	Low	Low	5

Risk management custodians at all levels are responsible for managing the process and related decision support activities at their respective levels.

Use the uncertainty registers to manage information and action

Risk management custodians at all levels are responsible for managing the process and related decision support activities at their respective levels. Accordingly, each custodian must exercise a single-point control over the uncertainty register(s) at his level(s). Figure 7.1 illustrates one approach, which expands day-to-day participation in the identification of risk and opportunity-generating uncertainties whilst maintaining control over the inventory of uncertainties through single-point screening.

The benefit of the approach shown is that it facilitates individual submissions of additional significant uncertainties as they are discovered, rather than limiting identification to formal brainstorming, interviews and periodic reviews. A member of the implementation team who identifies a particular significant uncertainty simply enters it into an electronically accessible 'uncertainty hopper' for screening by the custodian.

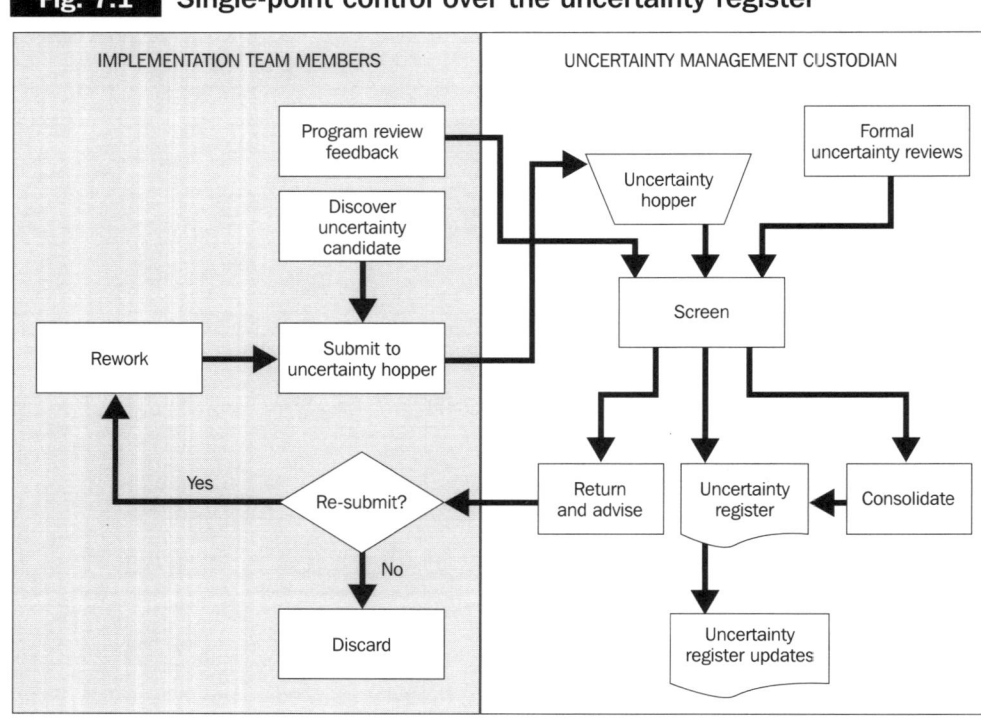

Fig. 7.1 Single-point control over the uncertainty register

Commencement of implementation brings into prominence the role of the uncertainty register as an action management tool.

Formal feedback of screened and accepted uncertainty candidates to the implementation team takes place through scheduled register update issues, although the register is updated continually and available to the implementation team at all times through electronic access.

In practice there will be a hierarchy of registers. Figure 7.2 depicts the:

- various levels of uncertainty registers corresponding to the levels of management during implementation;

- upward feed of information of concern to higher management levels;

- downward communication of higher management priorities.

At contract and sub-contract management levels the registers are denoted in the diagram as risk registers. This is a recognition, for the sake of illustration, that the contractual relationship often incentivises the contractor to manage risks he shares in common with the customer, but not to manage opportunities emanating from uncertainty. The greater the alignment of contractor incentives with his customer interests, the more his register will reflect the same management priorities as those evidenced in his customer's uncertainty register.

Commencement of implementation brings into prominence the role of the uncertainty register as an action management tool. In this role it provides a crucial link between different levels of management and various participation on organisations during implementation. It serves as a vehicle for:

- allocating responsibilities for, and actioning, management measures to deal with specific uncertainties and their influences;

- monitoring and reporting progress of those measures and their effects.

Fig. 7.2 **Communication between uncertainty registers during implementation**

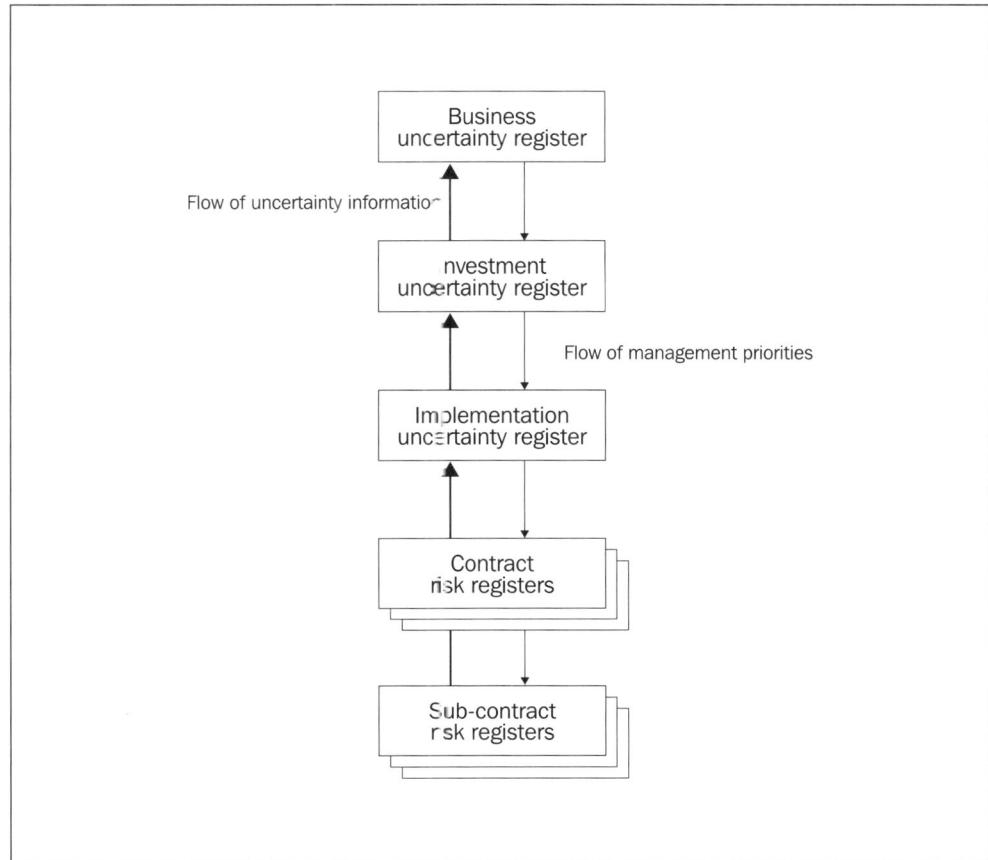

Like the hierarchy of uncertainty registers, there should also be a hierarchy of risk models throughout implementation. Both make a vital contribution to consistency of decision-making.

Use the risk models to monitor prospects and support consistent decision-making

Like the hierarchy of uncertainty registers, there should also be a hierarchy of risk models throughout implementation. Both make a vital contribution to consistency of decision-making between various management levels and between participating organisations. The risk management plan for the implementation stage needs to have specified adequate requirements for risk modelling to ensure that consistency. In particular, procedures should specify that:

■ all risk models reflect the following, in their logic and variable estimates:

– current work plans, cost and resourcing plans and investment/business plans;

– modellable uncertainties, as described in the uncertainty registers for the equivalent level;

– available current knowledge, both documented and undocumented;

■ the use of the following results in consistent investment, overall schedule and overall cost modelling:

– integrated risk models that carry incomes, durations, costs and key limiting resources, with variable logic and estimates and modellable interrelationships;

– documented linking between schedules and cost risk models to depict effects of time-dependent cost, and between these models and the investment model to depict the influence of time variability as well as cost variability;

■ schedule and cost modelling are consistent between levels of management (e.g. programme, project, sub-project, work package), through either manual or software linking.

The risk management custodians should manage the risk models used at their respective levels for quantitative risk analysis as well as looking after the uncertainty registers. This enables them to effect the mapping of uncertainties from the registers to the models, and to reflect key assumptions in the modelling. The resultant consistency between registers and models helps to ensure a reliable means of testing proposed implementation strategies, actions and decisions for their ranges of possible cost/benefit trade-off.

Figure 7.3 re-visits the risk management cycle to highlight the four possible outcomes (at lower right), which emerge from monitoring and control. Both new uncertainties and risks which have not been managed to plan are subjected to quantitative modelling:

■ to assess their influences on overall investment and work scope performances;

■ to assess the effects of proposed action plans for managing them.

The testing of action plans, by means of quantitative risk modelling, is depicted in the upper right corner of the diagram as a loop including re-cycling through the planning step to refine the action plan before its acceptance for execution.

The reiteration of this management cycle, with its quantitative risk analysis, tends to be more frequent, and the level of activity more intensive, during implementation than at any other stage in the investment life. Frequency of reiteration depends somewhat on the sensitivity of investment and business goals to the achievement of implementation targets. Frequency of reiteration also often mirrors the level of project activity or spend.

Fig. 7.3 The risk management process as an iterative cycle

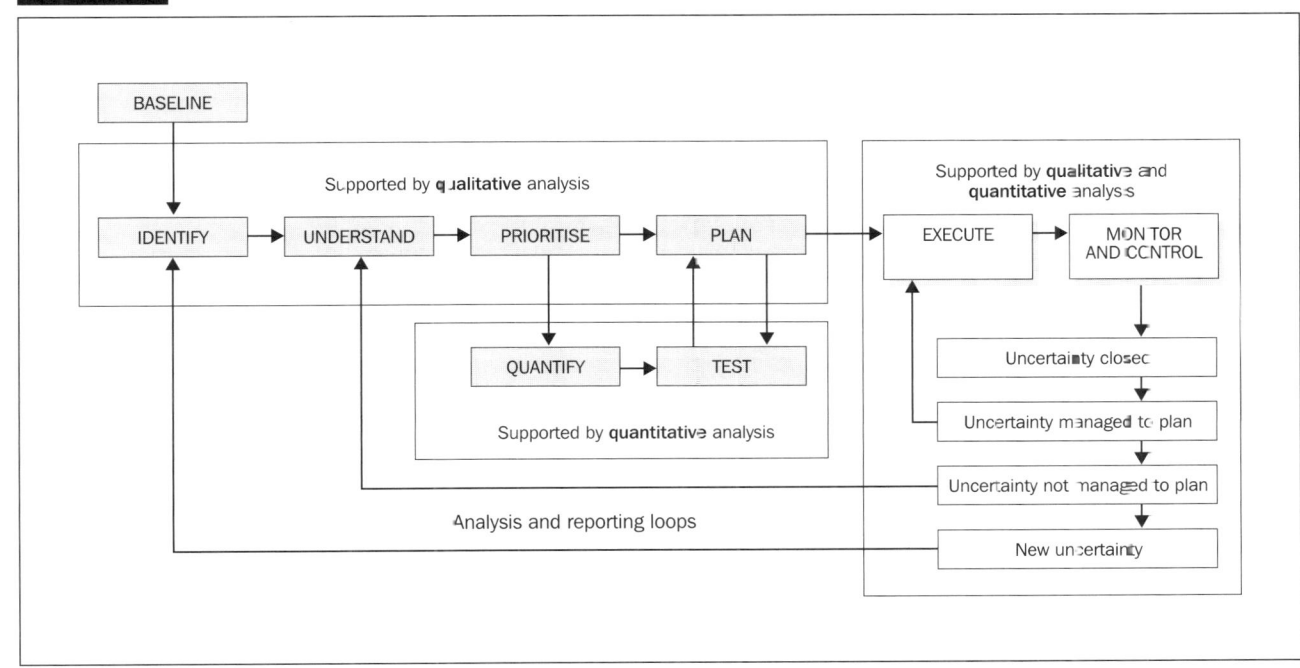

Integrate with project management

Whether or not a project management plan was prepared to govern the conduct of D&P work, there will be such a plan for the implementation stage. Furthermore, the direct consequences of project performance to achievement of investment and, in some cases, business goals make the management of implementation uncertainty and its influences indispensable to project decision-making, progress monitoring and control.

Implementation therefore needs to integrate risk management (already operating in conjunction with value management) with project management. The management plans prepared during project development and planning should have provided the procedural mechanisms for this. Figure 7.4 depicts the basic procedural and information links that effect this integration. The implementation risk log is a chronicle of analysis, reporting, executive decisions and actions, and results concerning the management of uncertainty and its influences throughout the implementation stage. Its function is to provide a permanent record for diagnosis of decision-making on the project and for the capture of lessons learned to benefit future projects.

Fig. 7.4 Procedural and information system links to integrate project management and risk management

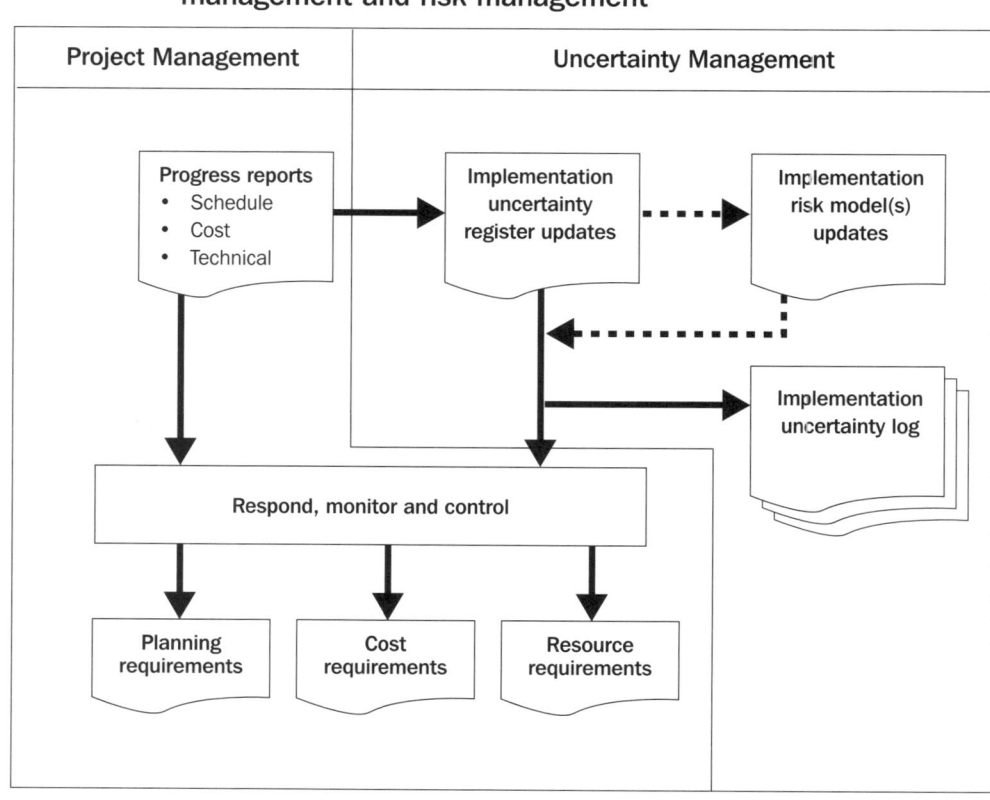

The procedural effects of integrating risk management with project management are that uncertainty registers and implementation risk models are used to:

- establish management priorities for dealing with project risks and opportunities;
- formulate strategies and actions for managing risks and opportunities;
- set challenging but achievable targets;
- develop master plans and programmes that satisfy requisite certainty levels on those targets;
- monitor target prospects, risks and opportunities for aggressive management;
- single-value plans and budgets based on the results of uncertainty analysis are used for tasking and progress reporting purposes.

The practical effects of integrating risk management with project management should be significant. However, if the added value from evaluation is not followed up with executive action, the beneficial effects will be lost to the project.

In Chapter 6, we saw that the guidelines on setting of implementation targets offered a graphical example of combined time and cost targeting, using targets incorporated within the lower half of possible outcomes. Figure 7.5 shows an example of using the 'expected' (average expectancy) time and cost out-turns as the targets. This is more representative of targets used in risk and gain-sharing arrangements for apportionment of overrun costs and better-than-targeted performance benefits. Figure 7.6 shows the prospects updated several time units later. What it should depict is progress in dealing with uncertainty. What it demonstrates, instead, is a deterioration of certainty levels on both time and cost targets.

- Uncertainty (i.e. the size of the 'cat's eye') has not diminished with time as 'possibles' have become 'actuals'.

- The universe of possible performance has moved upward in cost and outward in time.

Both trends are symptomatic of either one or a combination of:

- failure to initially identify major risks;

- failure in actioning, monitoring and controlling uncertainty management measures;

- intervention by truly unforeseeable adversities.

Fig. 7.5   Targets for risk and gain sharing

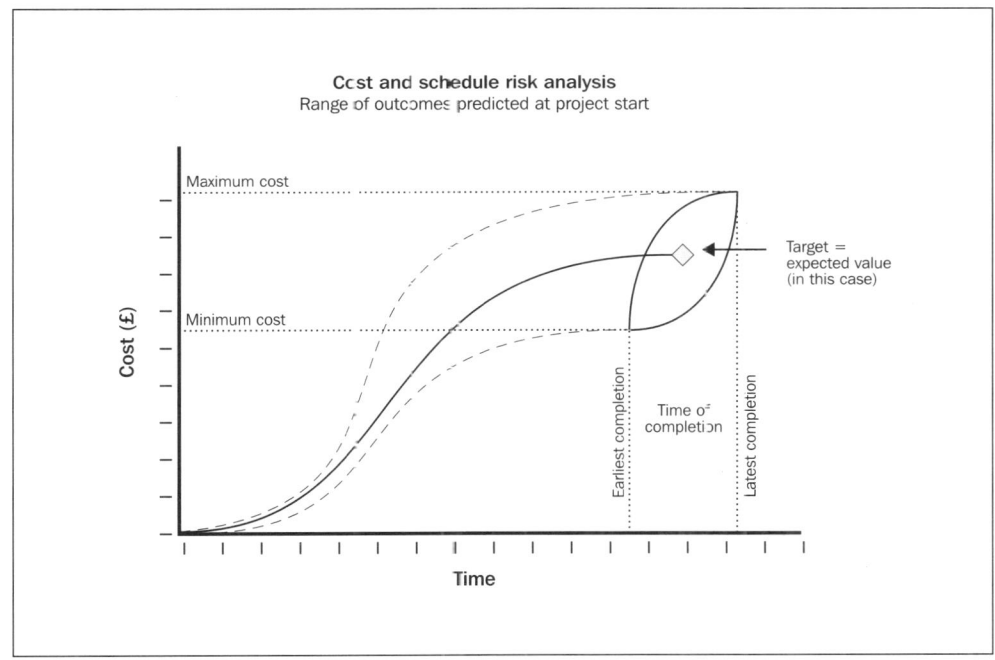

Fig. 7.6 Updating progress?

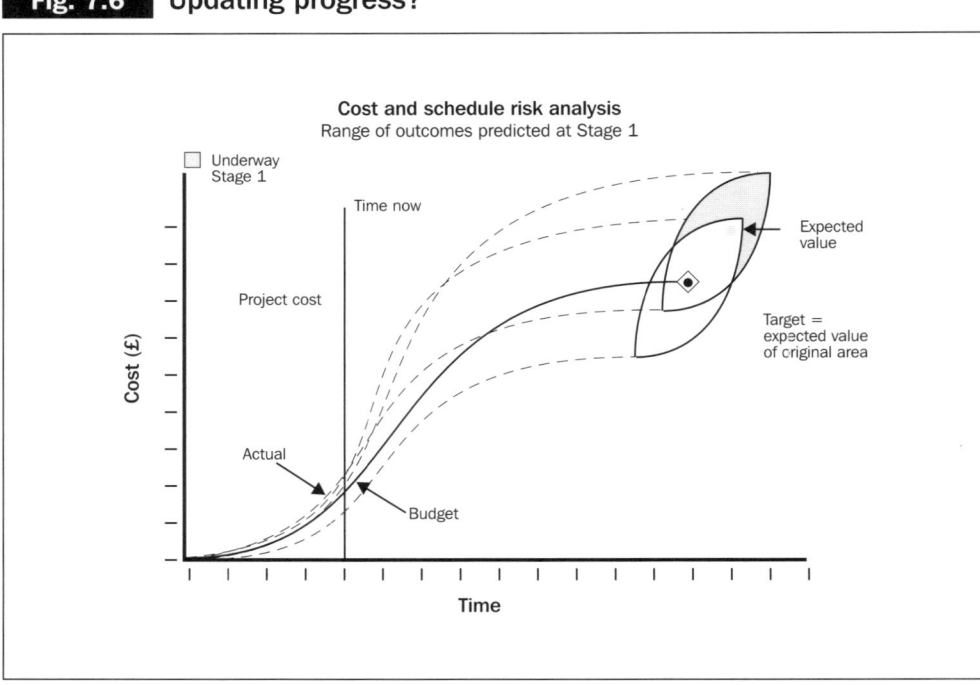

Eventually most possibles become actuals. The situation depicted above, if allowed to continue unchecked, can easily deteriorate beyond the point where originally realistic targets arrived at through rigorous analysis of uncertainties become unachievable. Figure 7.7 demonstrates a corrective application of risk management where the trend indicated in Figure 7.6 has been corrected. Uncertainty has diminished with time, and the universe of possible performance has moved downward and to the left.

Plan for operations and divestment

Implementation typically consists of delivering a capital asset, which will then commence a revenue/benefit-earning life. It is customary project practice for the team that will take possession of that asset to be represented, along with business management, throughout much of the implementation stage at all critical review and strategic decision points. Participation of operations management becomes increasingly active as implementation nears completion.

Fig. 7.7   Paradise gained

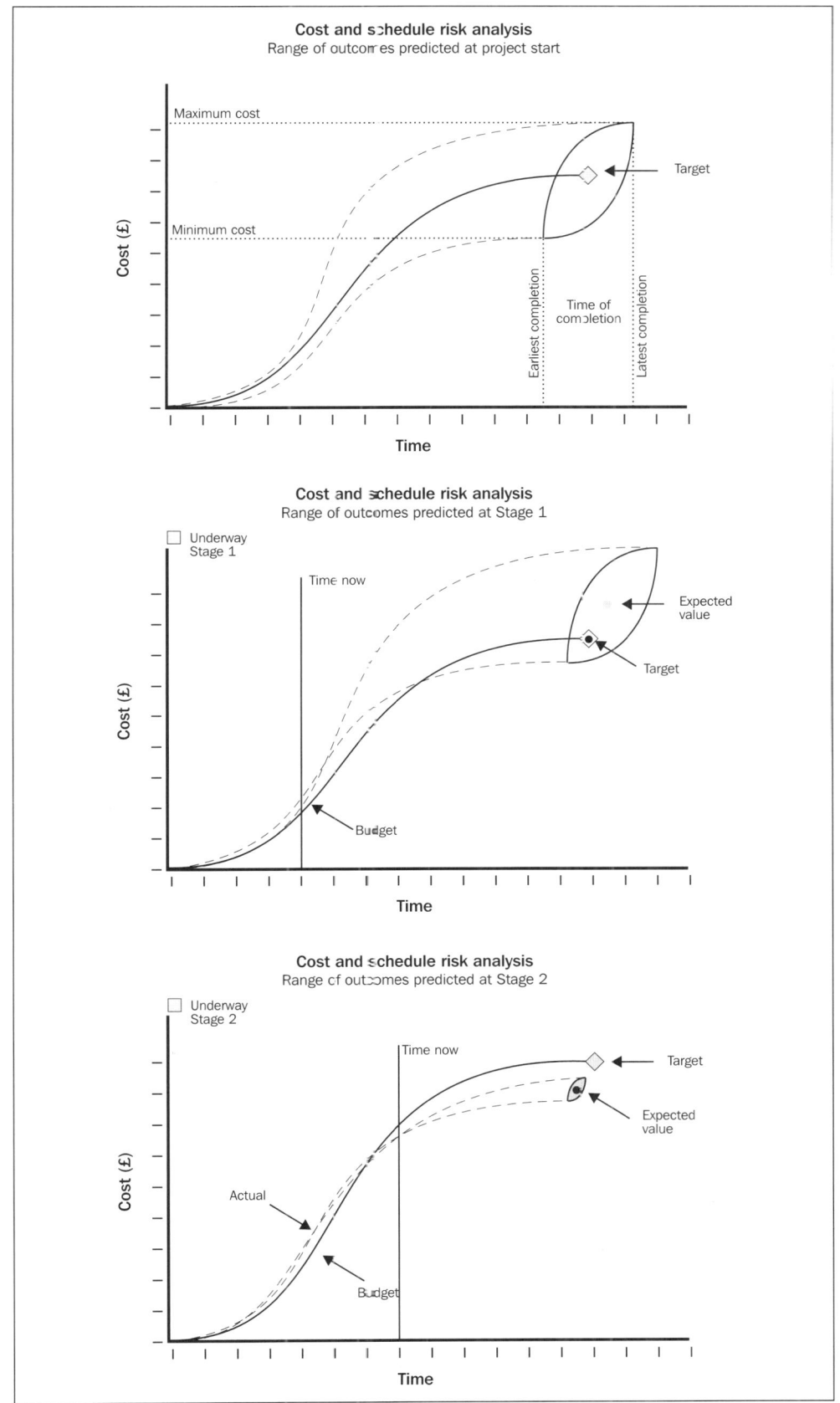

Planning for operations and divestment will comprise activities within the implementation masterplan which are carried out by operations or business management representatives. These include:

- development of acceptance criteria and plans for acceptance and handover;

- development of operations plans and budgets, possibly distinguishing between phases from start-up to steady-state;

- finalisation of related operations stage plans and budgets, such as those for marketing and sales, distribution, integrated logistics, customer support and disaster recovery;

- definition of divestment scenarios with associated costs and/or residual values.

All of this planning needs to reflect the uncertainties which lie ahead for the investment scheme and their influences on future performances. Just as risk management supported the previous stage's planning for the implementation stage, it is now essential to ensuring the smooth handover and transition from implementation to the operation.

PRE-OPERATIONS INVESTMENT REVIEW

All of the plans for operations and divestment need to be reviewed for the influence of uncertainty, risk and opportunity before the sanctioning of operations plans and budgets. This review, like that which preceded implementation authorisation, should:

- take into account the effects, on the business case, of any significant changes to the assumptions used in project development and planning that might have taken place during implementation;

- take into account any significant changes to investment or business objectives which might have occurred;

- update and analyse the investment risk model to test ranges and confidence levels for investment performance;

- scrutinise all the operations stage planning, with proposed schedules, phasing and budgets.

HANDOVER TO OPERATIONS

Implementation is only complete for handover to operations management when the asset delivered is accepted. At the point where handover takes place business management presides over the authorisation of operations based on the latest investment review. At this final stage:

- business and investment objectives and priorities are confirmed;

- any changes required by business management to operations stage planning are agreed with the operations management team and other business functions, as appropriate;

- schedules and budgets are ratified;

- handover from the implementation stage team to the operations team takes place.

CHAPTER REVIEW

- Protection of whole-life interests during implementation requires active management of investment and business uncertainty, unbiased by limited interests of implementation management. Broader investment and business priorities will predominate through:
  - contractual alignments between ability to influence, responsibility to manage and ownership of consequence;
  - alignments between incentives and investment and business objectives;
  - superior knowledge of uncertainties, their solutions and progress in their management.

- The critical bridge between all preceding work and implementation is the early confirmation of investment and implementation scopes and objectives.

- Risk management should support directly each management level it serves, not via general service functions, but through management of the overall process, and its application needs to be ultimately accountable to business management.

- Custodianship of risk management should have single-point control over the uncertainty registers and risk models at each level of management it serves.

- Development and testing of acceptance, handover, operations and divestment strategies, and operations plans and budgets, using uncertainty analysis, are the groundwork for ensuring value delivery after implementation.